We dedicate this book to:

MARY HARDAWAY GRIFFITH

*Who taught us how to do the
things we don't know how to do
to learn how to do them.*

Introduction

If we received a nickel for every time someone said to us, "You two should write a book," we'd have quite a sum saved by now. Yet selecting the right content and appropriate timing was essential. Many topics have crossed our minds during the 27 years we ve worked together (six years job sharing and 21 years founding/co-owning a corporate sustainability and governance consulting firm). But none seemed fitting for our first book—until we were given a unique and prized opportunity through the support of our good friend Beth Mooney, Chair and CEO of KeyCorp. What better way to "pay it forward" than to interview and share the uplifting stories of 25 top-ranking women executives—about those who lifted them up on their journeys and those they uplifted along the way?

Don't get us wrong—our book isn't just a collection of warm and fuzzy narratives. Rather, the women featured, spanning a variety of industries and, age-wise, nearly three decades, tackled their share of challenges. In the face of adversity, they persevered. Often the minority, they prevailed. Pressured to succeed in many "firsts," they triumphed. Their winding roads to success were paved with unexpected detours and encounters, both by those wanting to lift them up and others wishing to knock them down. Even so, the encounters that stand out most for all the women were about those who provided support when they needed it most, and often that support came from men.

Yet, one hard fact remains: while women in the workforce have evolved and gained ground over the years, there still exists a large gap at the top. Of the 2016 Fortune 500 companies, just 21 are led by women, down from 24 last year. Reversing this trend won't happen overnight. However, we challenge you to reflect on the stories and advice shared in our book to determine what actions you can take—either in your homes or your workplaces—to drive a "liftoff" of more women to the top. To this end and in celebration of BrownFlynn's 20th anniversary, we will donate all of our book's net proceeds to support the young women transitioning out of foster care through the YWCA Greater Cleveland's NIA program—Nurturing Independence and Aspirations—in furthering their education. We believe there is no better way to lift up one's self-esteem *and* career than a good education and following the valued insights in this book.

Please join us in "paying it forward" and passing on these uplifting stories.

BARB BROWN AND MARGIE FLYNN
Co-Founders and Principals, BrownFlynn

Uplifting Leaders*

*Who Happen To Be Women

Barbara O. Brown and Margaret P. Flynn

Published by BrownFlynn Ltd., Cleveland, Ohio

Published by BrownFlynn Ltd., 50 Public Square, Terminal Tower, 36th Floor, Cleveland, Ohio 44113

ISBN 978-0-692-81794-0

Printed in the United States of America

First printing

Foreword by Beth Mooney, Chair and CEO, KeyCorp

I met Margie Flynn and Barb Brown within the first few months after I moved to Cleveland to become Vice Chair of KeyCorp just over 10 years ago. Barb and Margie were among a group of executive women who attended my "welcome to Cleveland" party. It's no coincidence that, similar to the women featured in this book, we were surrounded by women who clearly cared for and supported one another both personally and professionally. My friendship with Margie and Barb and many of the other women that began that night has been enduring, and I am privileged to write the foreword to Margie and Barb's book about leaders who happen to be women.

Uplifting Leaders is a collection of stories about women leaders in business who, at various stages in their professional careers, have broken through glass ceilings. The book dives into the qualities these woman leaders embody that have both accelerated their careers and the companies they so proudly represent. These woman embody being authentic, positive, resilient, focused, and purposeful. They are passionate, inclusive, prepared, and accountable in the work that they lead. They create diverse and inclusive teams that are vision-oriented, and willing to learn and adapt to the rapidly changing demands of the modern business world. These women are not satisfied with simply gaining their own success, but they lift up others by listening to and coaching young leaders along the way.

The book provides insights into leaders across a diverse set of industries and unveils common qualities which demonstrate the character and integrity of good leadership. These qualities are what will propel a more diverse and gender-balanced workforce across industries and help the trailblazers identified in this book achieve their respective footnotes in their companies' histories. Furthermore, these qualities are not the property of women leaders, but leaders in general. Men in leadership roles can learn from the qualities highlighted in this book. The goal of *Uplifting Leaders* is to embrace the leadership qualities highlighted in this book so that both men and women have the potential of becoming exceptional leaders which, in turn, can create an exceptional business and simultaneously uplift those around them.

After reading *Uplifting Leaders,* I was reminded that leadership is an ongoing journey. Even as the chairman and CEO of KeyCorp, I continually learn from others. This book is chock-full of stories which, when taken to heart, contain an uplifting message to current or aspiring leaders at any stage of their professional career. I urge you to read on...

Meet Our
25
Interviewees

VIRGINIA ALBANESE
President and Chief Executive Officer,
FedEx Custom Critical

JODI L. BERG
President and Chief Executive Officer,
Vitamix Corporation

JENNIFFER D. DECKARD
President and Chief Executive Officer,
Fairmount Santrol

HEATHER ETTINGER
Managing Partner,
Fairport Asset Management

ADENA FRIEDMAN
President and Incoming
Chief Executive Officer, Nasdaq

SUSAN M. FUEHRER
Medical Center Director,
Louis Stokes Cleveland VA Medical Center

M. ANN HARLAN
Co-CEO, Harlan Peterson Partners, LLC; Retired,
Vice President and General Counsel,
The J.M. Smucker Company

CARLA HARRIS
Vice Chairman, Wealth Management,
Managing Director and Senior Client Advisor,
Morgan Stanley

E. LAVERNE JOHNSON
Founder, President, and Chief Executive Officer,
International Institute for Learning, Inc.

ERIKA KARP
Founder and Chief Executive Officer,
Cornerstone Capital Inc.

ROBIN M. KILBRIDE
President, Chief Executive Officer
and Chairman of the Board,
Smithers-Oasis Company

ILENE H. LANG
Former President and
Chief Executive Officer, Catalyst

BETH E. MOONEY
Chairman and Chief
Executive Officer, KeyCorp

DENISE MORRISON
President and Chief Executive Officer,
Campbell Soup Company

KAREN PARKHILL
Executive Vice President and
Chief Financial Officer, Medtronic

SANDRA PIANALTO
Former President and Chief Executive Officer,
Federal Reserve Bank of Cleveland

DR. JEAN ROGERS
Chief Executive Officer and Founder,
Sustainability Accounting Standards Board

MARCELLA KANFER ROLNICK
Vice Chair, GOJO

LISA SHERMAN
President and Chief Executive Officer,
The Advertising Council

BARBARA R. SNYDER
President, Case Western
Reserve University

DARLA STUCKEY
President and Chief Executive Officer,
Society for Corporate Governance

DR. JERRY SUE THORNTON
Chief Executive Officer,
Dream/Catcher Educational Consulting Service

LISA WOLL
Chief Executive Officer,
US SIF/US SIF Foundation

To learn more about this outstanding group of women executives, please refer to pages **87–96.**

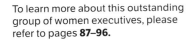

MARGARET W. WONG
Managing Partner,
Margaret W. Wong & Associates, LLC

JACQUELINE WOODS
Retired President,
AT&T Ohio

1

Lasting Impressions:
Uplifting Leaders
Carry Life Lessons

Most aspiring and accomplished leaders carry with them valuable life lessons that go well beyond textbooks and classrooms. In direct and subtle ways, the people who surround us throughout our lives leave lasting impressions that shape who we become. For our leaders' generation, they learned by example from family, extended family, and positive influencers who uplifted them through words (sometimes peppered with hard doses of reality) and inspirational actions.

Charity Begins at Home

The lessons learned as children extend well into corporate leadership. Virginia Albanese, president and CEO, FedEx Custom Critical, grew up in a family where giving to the community was a way of life. As a child, Virginia lived in England, and her mother took the children to local events to benefit their neighbors. "My mother always told us, 'Charity begins at home,'" she says. "Every year, there was a 'sports day' at a home for mentally and physically challenged children. We'd go and join the games to make things more fun for those kids. My mother also ran a canteen on Sundays at a hospital, and I'd clear the tables or pour tea. This was a wonderful way of teaching us the value of caring for others." At FedEx Custom Critical, Virginia has instilled this same commitment to community in the company's culture, and employees greatly value the opportunity to get involved.

In much the same way, Jenniffer Deckard, president and CEO, Fairmount Santrol, learned about community responsibility firsthand. Instead of going *out* to help others, her mother often brought people *in*. "We always had an extra person in the house," Jenniffer says. "We didn't have a lot of money, but if anybody was in need, my mother put a roof over their head. When a teenage girl of our acquaintance became pregnant, her parents put her out of their home. My mom's reaction was to invite her to live with us. She stayed even after the baby was born, as part of the family." Another experience stands out: "One cold day, driving home from church, we saw an older lady with ragged gloves. Mom stopped the car, took off her own gloves and gave them to that lady on the street." Actions like these speak louder than words when it comes to imparting lessons about caring for others—lessons that Jenniffer has embraced throughout her career and which she has tried to carry with her as a leader and in the boardroom.

Similarly, Carla Harris, managing director and senior client advisor, Morgan Stanley, watched her mom take other children under her wing. "She always listened to them, and she never acted like it was an infringement on her time," she says. "She was one of the most educated moms on our block—she had a master's degree. Kids would often come by to talk and ask about college and money and their future. My mother was always willing to take time for them. That inspired me to do the same thing. Whenever someone wants to talk about their career with me, I always have an open door."

Jodi Berg, president and CEO, Vitamix, learned the importance of kindness and following the Golden Rule by example from her father, who preceded her in her business role. "My dad doesn't have a bad intention in his body," she says. "He could never be angry without a good reason, and I don't think he could ever hold a grudge. A day doesn't go by that I don't think of him as I strive to follow his example both at work and in my personal life."

"My mother was always willing to take time to listen. Whenever someone wants to talk about their career with me, I always have an open door."
CARLA HARRIS

Think Big, Get Strong, and Find a Way

Leaders know the value of hard work as their diligent parents set examples for them to follow. Karen Parkhill, executive vice president and CFO, Medtronic, describes her father's work ethic: "My dad is an amazing man and a great inspiration for hard work. He's brilliant and caring, and not only did he find a way to succeed, but he made sure his whole family did too. He was the oldest of five kids in Fargo, North Dakota. From the age of 12, he was the 'man of the family' and had to earn an income to support everyone. Despite all that adversity, he put himself through medical school and became a prominent orthopedic surgeon. Along the way, he helped all four of his siblings through college and graduate school. My goal is to apply the same work ethic he taught me to benefit others."

Dr. Jerry Sue Thornton, CEO, Dream/Catcher Educational Consulting Service, had confident parents who inspired her to live by the motto, *Find a way.* "Neither of my parents went to high school," she says, "but they encouraged all five of their children to keep learning. When we graduated high school, Dad said, 'This is the best I can do, but if you're as smart as you think you are, you'll find a way to go to college.' So I did. I paid my college tuition by making costumes for the drama department and working in the cafeteria—breakfast, lunch, and dinner. I often fell asleep in class, and one day my English professor chastised me about having too much of a social life. '*What* social life?!' I asked him. But other teachers saw how hard I was working and pushed me to think even bigger."

Adena Friedman, President and incoming Chief Executive Officer, Nasdaq, credits her parents as role models who showed her firsthand the rewards of hard work. "My father spent his entire career at T. Rowe Price, and in the last 10 years on the job, he was their chief investment officer. When school was out, I had the good fortune to visit his office and watch him work with the traders. That was memorable and fun for me. He worked extremely hard and was revered by many. When I was nine, my mom started law school and, on occasion, I was able to go to school with her. In fact, I was once a witness in a mock trial. At other times, I sat in the back of the classroom, so I had the opportunity to see the competitiveness and rigor of that environment. I had a sense of what it took for her to pass the bar exam, and I watched her career unfold after having been a stay-at-home mom. She eventually became the first woman partner in her firm. And most of the time, she still made dinner for us. It was kind of incredible."

A hero is someone who sees no obstacles or at least has a plan for working around them. For Jenniffer Deckard, that hero and role model was her mother. Jenniffer's mom was widowed in her early twenties and had four children to raise. "But my mom's story wasn't sad," she says. "It was amazing. And somehow, I always felt that there was nothing beyond my reach, ever. I never thought, 'Could I go to college?' or 'Could I do that kind of work?' Rather, I simply decided to go to college and be an accountant. And that's just what I did."

Inspiring a Positive Outlook on Life

"Family" can extend beyond biological boundaries. And often, those who are in our lives to inspire us stay quietly in the background until we need them most. At one point in her life, Robin Kilbride, president, CEO, and chairman of the board, Smithers-Oasis, had a great career, but she doubted whether she was using her gifts and talents in the best way. "I talked to my minister's wife," she recalls, "and she said I was wrong. She told me, 'You have the ability to influence and touch so many people!' That simple statement inspired me—it made me look at what I could do in a totally different way. We forget that we don't all have to be in service industries to make an impact. How we conduct ourselves at work can make a huge difference in people's lives."

"My mother gave me confidence, the ability to see the glass half full, and the desire to make people around me better."

DARLA STUCKEY

A positive presence can shape an individual's approach toward life in general. Darla Stuckey, president and CEO, Society for Corporate Governance, says, "My mother gave me confidence, the ability to see the glass half full, and the desire to make people around me better."

Inspiration can come in familiar packages or in unexpected ways. The key is to know it when you see it or hear it, then remember it. True leaders realize the need to pass it on, to set that butterfly effect into motion, and to become the ones who will uplift someone else down the road.

A Full Circle of Inspiration

E. LaVerne Johnson, founder, president, and CEO, International Institute for Learning, was lucky. She had an extended family who supported her from the start.

> I was the fourth child of seven, kind of lost in the middle, and my aunt, who had no children, took it upon herself to just *listen* to me for as long as I wanted to talk about anything at all. No one had ever done that for me! My aunt made me believe that I could achieve anything. I also had an uncle who was a contractor with his own company, and he helped me understand what owning a business was all about—relationships, trust, delivering on time and within budget, cash flow, making payroll, and being proud of what you produce.
>
> When I started my own business, my mother showed up on day one, helping to stuff envelopes. She stayed with us as the "voice of the company" until she died at 95. Everything I've ever done was to make her proud of me. Maybe the most valuable advice I got came from my grandfather, who worked for years on the Frisco Railroad: "*Be true to yourself.*"

Aiming High as a Way of Life

For Denise Morrison, president and CEO, Campbell Soup Company, the drive for high standards started around the dinner table.

> My father had a training program that we kids didn't know we were going through. It included grades. A "C" always brought the comment, "I know you can do better," which made us feel even worse than getting that "C". The words "I can't" were banned. Instead, we asked, "How can I...?" My dad would tell his four girls, 'The world is going to open up for women, and I want you to be ready for it.'" (*Note: Denise's sister Maggie Wilderotter is CEO of Frontier Communications.*)

From her father, Denise learned the importance of routine, self-discipline, and learning—which set her up for success simply because she became used to achieving high expectations. His inspiration didn't stop when Denise reached the top. She says:

> I remember when I called my parents and said, "Mom! Dad! I did it! I'm the CEO of Campbell Soup!" There was a pause, and my father said, "That's great, Denise. We're proud of you. What's your next goal?" And I said, "To build a great company."

2

Lifelong Learners:
Uplifting Leaders
Listen and Learn

The wise man Yogi Berra once said, "You can observe a lot just by watching." In the same vein, our wise leaders agree you can learn a lot just by listening, and you can use what you learn to uplift others. Good listening is a rare talent, and there are benefits to choosing silence at the proper times.

Encourage Others to Speak

Karen Parkhill cites an old saying—"God gave us two ears and one mouth. Use them in proportion." When you do that, she says, "You hear what's needed and which course corrections to make."

Susan Fuehrer, Medical Center director, Louis Stokes Cleveland VA Medical Center, learned a lesson from her predecessor who told her, "You know, Sue, you might be the smartest person in the room, and everyone might *think* you're the smartest person in the room, but you don't need to *prove* it. You don't have to be the first to come to a conclusion, because when you listen to others, you learn a whole lot."

In some circumstances, you may have to convince people that it's safe to voice their opinions. If that's the case, a leader needs to give people encouragement to do so. "Let them know you want to hear what they have to say," says Karen Parkhill. "Be sure they know you're on a path of continual improvement for the business and their thoughts are important."

"Let them know you want to hear what they have to say—that their thoughts are important."

KAREN PARKHILL

When people have the chance to speak freely, especially in a group that includes executives or their managers, it affords them an opportunity to assess their ideas more clearly and actually *be heard.* Dr. Jerry Sue Thornton believes it "helps people think things through simply by listening to them, as it can be easier to understand what we think when we hear ourselves say it aloud."

Often, great ideas are limited to lunchroom chats that leaders never hear. To bring those ideas into the open, Heather Ettinger, managing partner, Fairport Asset Management, recommends creating a safe environment where people feel free to voice their ideas and taking time to be sure everybody gets heard. One of Heather's favorite ways to do this includes the process "ERRC," which stands for Eliminate, Reduce, Raise, and Create. After a client meeting or reviewing project strategies, she asks others for feedback on what she should be doing less of or eliminating altogether. She then asks what she should be doing more of or creating to improve processes, client experience, or job effectiveness. She says, "A critical part of this process is to recognize the less effective choices that you as a leader have made and demonstrate how you learned from them so others know it's possible to give you constructive feedback. In turn, it gives them permission to ask for what they need to change or improve to do their jobs better. Everyone gets to participate, and I applaud particularly the most daring and thoughtful feedback. Leaders must model the behavior that they want from others."

When You Listen, Your Company Gains

All our leaders consider their workplaces "schools" where they continually learn from other people and situations, and pass that learning on to others. When leaders listen, the people they are listening to and the company itself both win. Those who genuinely listen can use what they hear to help people improve their lives and careers.

Because individuals interpret things differently, listening allows you to inspire them in meaningful ways, according to Jodi Berg. "If I'm going to uplift people, to inspire them to discover how they can make a difference on the planet," she says, "I have to listen to them to learn who they are and what they respond to. Only then can I help them discover that knowledge in themselves."

Jackie Woods, retired president, AT&T Ohio, says her leadership style morphed from control-and-command to one that's consensus-building, and listening has been a big part of that transition. She says, "I'm listening and considering alternatives instead of saying, 'This is what we should do.'"

Interestingly, when it comes to being good listeners, women may have a subtle advantage. Adena Friedman believes women are intrinsically good listeners because they are generally more empathetic. She recommends using that skill as much as possible. "When you listen and try to see deeply into the psyche of your client or employee, you can gain a deeper understanding of what needs to be done to improve the product or your relationship or the company," she says.

Well-developed listening skills add to your worth as a leader even when the outcome doesn't satisfy someone's specific request. Lisa Woll, CEO, US SIF/US SIF Foundation, says, "Part of your effectiveness is hearing what people need or desire from you, figuring out how much of that you can meet, and then communicating in a way that shows you understand. This makes them feel they've been heard, respected, and included—even if you can't do all they're asking you to do."

By watching others, Jenniffer Deckard learned the importance of giving constructive feedback, even when it's painful to hear: "I have noticed that good leaders recognize the importance of honest feedback and have learned how to give that feedback with clarity, patience, and kindness, even when—or especially when—that needed feedback is on the critical side. By avoiding constructive feedback, you're not saving that person from the critique. Rather, you're making the choice to forego *uplifting* that person to higher levels."

You can't drive change by yourself—that's a lesson Karen Parkhill learned from others. "You create the right environment that will encourage people and make them want to do better, not destroy their motivation. I focus on setting the bar high, chinning it, and raising it again." Lisa Woll has learned that most people don't spend the necessary amount of time thinking about *how* they're going to lead. "By really listening to yourself and thinking about how you want to lead, that's how you increase your effectiveness," she says. "It's important to put in the effort."

Learning What Not To Do

There's another side to the learning coin. Knowing what *not* to do is just as important as knowing what *to do*, and if you can learn that lesson by listening to others, you can avoid a lot of pain. Ilene Lang, former president and CEO, Catalyst, says, "It's not just about what questions to ask. It's knowing what situations you shouldn't walk into." Erika Karp, founder and CEO, Cornerstone Capital, agrees. "I've learned so much about what not to do from many executives. It helps to just pay attention," she says.

Although good lessons can be learned from bad leaders, you first have to learn to distinguish between them, especially when you're starting a career. Beth Mooney, chair and CEO, KeyCorp, says, "Bad leaders aren't all inherently *bad,* but they serve as examples of behaviors you want to avoid. I've had a couple of chapters in my book of life—I'll call them 'profiles in courage'—where you find yourself in a situation with a boss or a leader who you weren't necessarily aligned with or didn't agree with how they ran or managed things. But I've learned from and grown a lot from experiences with leaders like that."

Susan Fuehrer tells her people that they can learn from good leaders, but sometimes they can learn a lot more from *bad* leaders "because you find out what you *don't* want to do or be."

One lesson Jackie Woods learned *not* to do was keeping an employee when they are not performing. Jenniffer Deckard agrees: "I've learned that getting the wrong people *off* the bus at the right time is an important but challenging leadership skill."

Attempting new things can be risky, and when you're a leader, you generally don't purposely invite failure. But some of our leaders have learned otherwise—that there's an upside. Darla Stuckey says, "I learned by listening and observing that you sometimes have to fail in order to succeed. You have to be willing to consider failures in different ways. You don't learn if you're immediately successful."

Listening as a Gift

When all the aspects of listening and learning are taken into consideration, they could be described as uplifting gifts—to those who listen and those who speak. In an increasingly busy world, time is one of the rarest gifts. Dr. Jean Rogers, CEO and founder, Sustainability Accounting Standards Board, expresses it like this: "Time is the most precious commodity that leaders have to give, in terms of listening and making sure people know we care about them. I really try to give them time."

"You sometimes have to fail in order to succeed. You don't learn if you're immediately successful."

DARLA STUCKEY

The benefits of listening come even closer to home—to leaders themselves, who need people to listen to *them* as well. Darla Stuckey says, "It can be very lonely at the top. Leaders need a trusted colleague, friend, or mentor to confide in." Beth Mooney agrees: "You need somebody who helps you realize your aspirations, understand what it takes to be successful, and show you how to develop personally and professionally."

Leaders often find themselves in groups that require them to listen to others' ideas but also present their own—to be listened to *themselves*. At times, this may require a thick skin.

Barbara Snyder, president, Case Western Reserve University, says, "Really good leaders can tolerate vigorous, robust discussions. I like to be challenged. People—bosses and employees—have often told me, 'I think you're wrong.' You have to be brave and open enough to accept that kind of feedback and invite it from everybody around you."

Learning as a Way of Life

Our leaders concur—when we stop learning, we stop growing. When we stop applying what we've learned, we become stagnant. In the end, the best reward may be using our knowledge to uplift others. Jackie Woods says, "The finest moment is when I can take something that I learned, assess it against where we are and what we need now, and make a good decision."

Like all our leaders, Barbara Snyder seeks opportunities to learn every day. She says it's one of the best things about her job. "I wanted to be a faculty member because I enjoyed being a student," she says. "When you're working on a college campus, you're constantly learning. I know it's true in the corporate world, too. In the best corporations, there's a push for continual learning and improvement—finding out how we can always do something better."

"I've passed my love of learning on to young people," says E. LaVerne Johnson. "I try to inspire them to accomplish great things and work for the betterment of the world—and I plan to keep on learning forever. I'm fortunate to be able to learn every day from our people. They are the experts at what they do, and I am their eager 'student.'"

No Elevator to the Top Floor

You can't wait until you get to the top of your career to begin learning how to be a leader, says Dr. Jerry Sue Thornton.

> My dad used to say, "There's no elevator to the top. It's one step at a time." So whenever I skip the elevator and take the stairs, I think about that. I say to myself, "It's one step at a time...one step at a time."

> To become a leader, you've got to be willing to take those steps—because if you don't, you'll miss a lot. You zoom to the top too fast. You get too heady. I believe this is something young professionals need to be mindful of—I'm not sure they see those steps. They're looking for the elevator. My advice to them? Every step makes you stronger.

Collecting Wise Thoughts

Robin Kilbride has been with her company for more than 30 years. She started as an analyst at age 24 and worked her way to the top, bringing lessons from great minds along the way.

> Early in my career, I had the privilege to be around a lot of great business leaders. I learned what works and what doesn't. I'm a note-taker, so if someone says something totally profound, I write it down. I have a "collection of wise thoughts" that goes back many, many years. And I remember the moments when someone has made a difference.

We all need to look for those learning moments—they can be such a positive influence on our lives.

Learning Before You Listen

Before people even speak, before they share an idea, a perceptive leader can learn, says Carla Harris:

> Once, when someone came to me for advice, my first reaction was, "I don't have time for this (based on what they were asking me)." But I think differently now. I stop and ask myself, "What did this person come to *teach* me?"

> When you're a leader, people come to you for a reason. There's something you need to know. You need to either learn about this personality type or how to ignore this particular issue and move past it, over it, or through it. But there's always some lesson you need to learn from this interaction. So change your script. Look at an "interruption" as something that could become valuable to you later.

3

Mentors:
Uplifting Leaders
Seek Out Support

No matter what your field or level of leadership, you've likely had some help along the way—someone who uplifted you by words and actions and encouraged you to grow. This help often comes in the form of a mentor.

Some mentors don't really "give advice." Their actions speak louder than words to prove they believe in you and respect you. The lessons are in everything they do. Other people can inspire you just by treating you with respect. These are the ones who never doubt that the choices you've made for yourself are the right ones. They bolster your self-confidence and help you forget any doubts that may be lingering in the shadows. Our leaders were fortunate to have benefitted from both kinds of mentors.

Getting Started with a Mentor

Before taking advantage of lessons from the outside, our leaders agree that the first thing to learn is *who you are*. Denise Morrison says, "If *you* don't know what you want to be, how can anybody help you?" Once you determine your own identity, it's important to find people who will model the right way to progress in your career life. "Most people think of a career like school—get a job, do it well, get promoted," she says. "But it really doesn't work that way. You have to build relationships and a network. It's like extracurricular activities or those extra assignments you raise your hand for. That's what will distinguish you as a leader."

Sometimes mentors find *you*, but more often you have to search to find the right fit. If that's the case, Dr. Jerry Sue Thornton recommends casting a wide net, maybe opting for people outside your usual circle.

When you've found the right mentor, the relationship doesn't have to be strictly business, but it helps to set some ground rules. When Jackie Woods started out, she was assigned a mentor, but she also recruited one on her own. After watching a senior leader in meetings and admiring how he managed to get things done while relating to others, she asked him to mentor her. When he agreed, she made three commitments to him: "I'll never ask you for a promotion or to help me get one. I'll never abuse your time. And I'll do my best to follow what you suggest."

That last point is a really important part of the relationship. Dr. Jerry Sue Thornton says, "Once you find your mentor, *listen*. Don't ask someone to serve as a role model and then ignore their advice. That's just wasting their time—and yours."

Without a guide, the path to success can be rougher than it needs to be. Margaret Wong, founder and president, Margaret W. Wong & Associates, didn't have a mentor early in her career.

"I had no one to tell me what I was doing wrong or why some people didn't seem to like me," she says. But there was an odd silver lining. She kept getting fired, which led her to start her own company. She wasn't alone, though, as she had good friends who helped her along the way—"people to talk to about my challenges—and my mom was a mentor to me later in life."

How the Best Mentors Teach

Mentors aren't just for back-patting and cheering you on. You can't learn from someone who doesn't tell you when you've gone off track, and a tough mentor is a good mentor. Barbara Snyder has had mentors who chose to avoid the naked truth. "I've had people tell me what they *think* I want to hear," she says. "I really want to know what the situation is and find a way to deal with it, even if it's ugly or hard."

Denise Morrison had a strong mentor early in her career, when she was the first woman in sales hired at Procter & Gamble. Her first district manager didn't pull any punches. "He believed in me," she says. "He nurtured my career, and he wanted me to be successful. But he was hard on me—which was good. "

Sometimes mentors teach in words, but more often, by example—how they operate under pressure, how they react to everyday situations, how they treat people at every level. Very often, these mentors are early bosses or predecessors.

Adena Friedman looked to her first boss at Nasdaq, Bill Broka, as her mentor. "He taught me to listen to the younger employees and not just surround myself with senior people. That's not something many leaders do well," she says. Broka also urged her to empower people and trust them to deliver, and that workplace flexibility is critical for creating a healthy environment. She adds one more thing: "Bill never yelled. He'd get stressed, but he'd keep his employees from feeling it. I try not to show stress, but project strength to our people, as he did."

Some mentors teach without words. Jenniffer Deckard says "My predecessors, Bill Conway and Chuck Fowler, led by example every day. They neither pontificated nor made big statements, but *showed* me by being humble, positive examples. In every major discussion, they talked about our people—what we could do better for them, or how a decision would affect them. I still ask myself, 'How would these men respond to that situation? Did I act as they would have done?"

Great mentors model leadership simply by being great leaders. Carla Harris learned valuable lessons from her mentor, Bob Scott, who was head of capital markets when she began working there and later became president and COO of Morgan Stanley. "Bob inspired everybody to contribute and own the outcome," she says. "He never asserted his will. He'd provoke a conversation and then gently guide it toward a beneficial conclusion."

Lisa Sherman, president and CEO, The Advertising Council, had two mentors who taught in different ways. "One was not your 'traditional' leader," she says. "He had great charisma, and he was an excellent speaker and presenter. He was always advocating for something—he talked about diversity before anybody else. He was willing to really shake things up, and I just adored him. You wanted to be around him because you felt better and were inspired when he was there. I thought, 'I'd like to have people react to me the way I'm reacting to him.' Another of my mentors was a very smart man who had great ideas of his own, but he'd always ask, 'What do you think?' and 'Let me know how I can help you.' He always had my back. He never told me what to do, but if I needed him, he was there. Something he told me sticks with me even today—'We have to use our superpowers for good.'"

> "'We have to use our superpowers for good.' That sticks with me even today."
> **LISA SHERMAN**

Some leaders who become mentors make a difference simply by their demeanor. Sandy Pianalto, former president and CEO, Federal Reserve Bank of Cleveland, considers one of her former bosses as a mentor. Karen Horn, one of her predecessors and the first woman president in the Federal Reserve System's 69-year history, taught her the power of composure. "I never saw Karen become frustrated or lose her cool," she says. "I didn't realize how much I'd learned from her until I became president and found myself in tough situations. Then I'd remember how *she* handled things and tried to do the same."

Mentors don't always show up at work; sometimes they appear in other settings. Marcella Kanfer Rolnick, vice chair, GOJO, found a mentor in Ruth Messinger of American Jewish World Service (AJWS). She says, "Through her own clarity of purpose and self-knowledge of her towering strengths, Ruth has inspired me to keep asking myself, 'What's my purpose? What change do I want to drive (since I can't do everything)?' to keep me from becoming complacent, diffused, or ineffective." By doing this, Marcella found where she could contribute her particular talents, which shaped her participation at her first AJWS board meeting: "I wanted to just listen and learn, so I didn't say a single word until the end of the second day. Then, I just couldn't help myself. I had to say *something*. I spoke up and made two valuable observations that led me to spearhead two major initiatives that really aligned with my strengths. This uplifting mentor drove home the timeless adage of 'know thyself.'"

Unexpected Mentors

Although most mentors are connected to work, they can appear almost anywhere if we're open and attentive. Ann Harlan, co-CEO, Harlan Peterson Partners, LLC; retired vice president and general counsel, The J. M. Smucker Company, says, "For me, a mentor is anyone I learn from. I believe we learn every day when we ask questions and are open to what others are saying and doing. I've learned perhaps the most from people who teach me in a quiet way, leading by example. Richard Smucker, for instance, is a leader who listens with his full attention and makes sure every voice in the room is heard. Tim Smucker, a true servant leader, always has the focus of the company's mission and values as his guiding principle, but he is never too busy to hear someone's idea. When there are visionary leaders at the top, everyone is encouraged to value their individual contribution and take risks to create positive change when they see the opportunity. When that kind of open leadership is present, new mentors and teachers come from unexpected places. One such unexpected person who taught me the value of always taking pride in my work was a woman who worked in the cafeteria line. She knew that doing her job well and with a smile made it easier for the rest of us to do our jobs well. She had ideas about how the cafeteria could be run more efficiently, and she spoke up. She made a difference in our days, and she taught us the value of a positive attitude. And isn't that what a mentor is, someone that changes us for the better?"

"For me, a mentor is anyone that I learn from. I've learned perhaps the most from people who teach me in a quiet way, leading by example."
ANN HARLAN

When we picture a mentor, we may think of those ahead of us on the path, but that limits the possibilities. "Wiser doesn't always have to be older," says Heather Ettinger, who has found teachers in the next generation of leaders, and often in her own children. "I've discovered things about them that I really admire. They're doing things I can't do, will never do, and wish I could do."

Anyone can be a mentor, whether the role is formal or not. Robin Kilbride counts many people in her life as mentors—people she didn't work *for*, but *with*: "They took time to explain things to me, listen to me, or ask me to join projects that I otherwise wouldn't have considered. They gave me opportunities to experience new things, and they were purposeful about that."

Many people try to find mentors they believe will relate to them, such as a young woman seeking an older, more experienced woman. But Jenniffer Deckard has found that's not always the case: "There is much written on women uplifting women, but my experience (outside of my amazing mother) has largely been that of men uplifting women. I've had relatively few female superiors. I have a terrific circle of supportive women to whom I can go for support, but for my entire career, my most influential professors and leaders were men. And nearly every single one uplifted me and gave me that next chance and that next opportunity."

Repay the Mentorship—Pass It On

Mentorship is a gift that requires us to respond in kind. Paying it forward is important, as mentors can be life-changing to anyone at any stage of life, and especially when it comes to growing leaders.

Margaret Wong has noticed a difference in what young people are looking for in a mentor. "Education and mentoring have always been very important to me," she says. "It's especially important for foreign-born children in America because they're at a disadvantage from the start. But mentoring is different today. Young people want to learn from you, but then go off on their own. I believe the younger generation has an opportunity to consider learning from our generation. In my day, we continually absorbed advice and hoped one day to give back as mentors ourselves."

Like many of the leaders in this book, Darla Stuckey had mostly male mentors, and she's not sure why that's true. "Either I didn't know how to ask, or I felt unworthy because I hadn't yet achieved anything. I had one great woman boss who made me feel wonderful. She gave me positive feedback after I'd received a lot of negative remarks. She made me feel important, and I wanted to do a good job for her. Today, I'm making a big push for more women to become mentors."

Gratitude is most often the motivator for returning the mentorship gift, says Robin Kilbride: "Because so many people created opportunities for me, I have a responsibility to create opportunities for others." Many of those who have been uplifted by a mentor feel a sense of duty to fill this role for other people. And there can even be a return on the investment. Denise Morrison benefitted from advice from mentors, but she knew it was a two-way street. "You need mentors to advance," she says, "but there's a quid pro quo—you give something to your mentors, too."

"Because so many people created opportunities for me, I have a responsibility to create opportunities for others."

ROBIN KILBRIDE

A Step Beyond Coaching

As a college athlete, Jenniffer Deckard found inspiring mentorship from her coaches. "Nearly all of my coaches have been men," she says. "And along the way, many uplifted me and gave me that next chance, that next opportunity."

She tells a story with which "women of a certain age" will identify—the pre-Title IX days when women's athletics was not a high priority.

> In college, there was practically no money for women's sports programs. My volleyball coach had to fight for every dime. When male athletes were on full scholarship and flying around the country in planes, our coach piled all 12 of us into a university van and drove us wherever we needed to go, from Texas to Tennessee. We were on a shoestring budget, but this man—who was also a full-time tenured professor with no need to do this—was committed to our sport and to each of us. He even did our laundry at night.

Accepting Your Own Success

When success arrives, we may need a bit of uplifting to accept that we not only *earned* it, but that we *deserve* it. That realization sometimes requires the perspective of a mentor.

Sandy Pianalto was vice president of the bank and in charge of public affairs and secretary to the board of directors when the Federal Reserve Bank's president called her to his office and invited her to sit down for a talk—a rather momentous talk.

> When he told me that the board wanted to appoint me chief operating officer, I almost fell off the sofa! I could barely believe it. After all, there were about 10 senior vice presidents ahead of me—all older men, all with operations experience. And do you know what I told him? I said *I didn't think I was qualified for the job* because I had no operations experience. Can you imagine a man sitting there and saying, "I'm not qualified"?
>
> I called Karen Horn, the bank's former president and my mentor, to tell her what happened and how I felt. I didn't get any sympathy from her—in fact, she was really upset with me. She said, "Sandy, stop it! *First*, get the job and *then* figure out how to do it."

So Sandy did just that. When someone believes in your abilities and has confidence in you, it's a bit easier to take that leap into the unknown.

"Everything I Know, I Learned from Someone Else"

Marcella Kanfer Rolnick has benefitted from a family of mentors. She credits her great-aunt and great-uncle as genuine models of ingenuity, inventiveness, and compassion.

I've always been encouraged by the example of my great-aunt and great-uncle who founded our company. The product that started it all, GOJO, the original heavy-duty hand cleaner, was invented in 1946 to solve an important human problem.

My great-aunt, Goldie Lippman, worked at a rubber factory during World War II. At the end of her shift, she found it nearly impossible to remove the grime from her hands. Chemicals worked but were rough on the skin. Out of concern for her co-workers and herself, Goldie and her husband, Jerome Lippman—my great-uncle—decided to create a better solution. With only a tenth-grade education and an audacious goal, Jerry asked for help from chemistry professor Clarence Cook at Kent State University. The result? A gentle, effective hand cleaner. And the name "GOJO"? It comes from their two first names, Goldie and Jerry. Whenever we talk about our company and our culture, we repeat something Jerry used to say all the time: "Everything I know, I learned from someone else." He understood the value of learning from people who know more than you do and who have hands-on experience, and he passed that lesson down through the generations of our family and our team members.

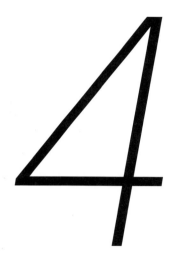

4

Trailblazing:
Uplifting Leaders
Create Their
Own Paths

The well-worn path, marked with arrows and signs, is the road most people take. It leads to the familiar, the comfortable, the safe. But stepping off that path has a certain allure. Just ask many of our leaders, or you might say "trailblazers." The urge to break away from the norm tempts adventurous people. It's exhilarating to be the first one to do something—*anything*. And while there are certainly some dangers, there are benefits as well, not to mention a heady feeling of personal accomplishment.

The unknown can be scary, according to Ilene Lang, who says, "When you're a trailblazer, there is no path. I never knew where anything might lead." But, she adds, there's a measure of freedom that comes with the unknown because there are no expectations. "It allowed for innovation," she says," because I had to find my own opportunities."

In the ongoing quest to uplift each other, there are challenges and rewards of going where no one's gone before.

Trailblazers: Are They Born or Made?

There may be a trailblazing gene. Some people seem to be born with a will to take steps into the unknown and make a difference in the world. Denise Morrison is one of those people—and she has proof. "I made a scrapbook when I was about eight years old," she says. "On the first page is my baby picture and these words, in my childhood handwriting: 'If I can do one thing to make the world a better place, my life would be worth it.' When I look at that now, I think how that goal really hasn't changed much."

Of course, if you're a born trailblazer, it may be easier than becoming one later on. You go through life assuming that every path ahead is one you'll forge for yourself. Heather Ettinger has never been afraid to try something new. "I was a pioneer in playing men's sports before that was the cool thing to do," she says, "and also in coming into the asset management industry when there were very few women in it. I was a pioneer in marketing asset management to women. To some degree, I was also a pioneer in leadership in our industry, where more than 90 percent of leaders are men." But she acknowledges that her success isn't totally due to her own self-confidence. She says, "I've succeeded because of the success around me."

Doing What Comes Naturally

There's no doubt that carrying life lessons is a plus when it comes to cultivating a trailblazer, as our leaders recounted in Chapter 1. Life lessons that come from generations of strong people, along with an expectation that *of course* you'll do well, goes a long way when it's time to enter the career world. Virginia Albanese was raised in a family like that, where no one was ever told they couldn't accomplish something. "My parents told me to try everything, to get every experience I could." She adds, "They'd say, 'You don't have to get married, but just be sure you can support yourself.'"

For some future trailblazers, there's never a question of limits. Jodi Berg had a mom who told her she could be anything she wanted to be. "I never questioned that," she says. "If I wanted to do it, I could do it."

Lisa Woll comes from an entire family of trailblazers, and they lit the spark of social awareness that led to her career in sustainable and impact investing: "I grew up in a culture of strong influences about social justice and community connections," she says. "My grandparents were trailblazers—Russian immigrants—and they were social activists in the labor movement. My parents were very involved in community affairs. I was very young during the social justice movements of the 1960s and '70s, but I remember them well. And I was certainly aware of women politicians as I grew up—people like Patricia Schroeder when she was in Congress. All of these were important influences."

Defying the Naysayers

Trailblazers don't always have cheerleaders. More often, they encounter people eager to warn them about their inability to fight the dragons ahead—even if they're fully armed with their own wits and abilities. You need more than just the will to blaze a trail, our leaders say. You need courage and fortitude. The real heroes believe in themselves and bravely stride down new paths.

Once you've proven the naysayers wrong, you may have a chance to clear the road for the next people on the path. Darla Stuckey did just that. When she first came to the Society for Corporate Governance as senior vice president, everyone reported to the CEO. After a change in leadership, she wasn't chosen as the new CEO because she'd had no management experience. The same thing happened a few years later. Finally, she earned that CEO position. Three senior women now report to her, and she has made sure they all have management responsibilities so they won't face the same challenge.

Taking a New Path Is Worth the Trip

Trailblazing isn't easy, but like working out, you get stronger as you go. Some benefits are about gaining influence and authority. Some are about empowering your own abilities.

You may need to tap lifelong strengths as you blaze new trails. You may not have considered these as business assets before, but that's certainly what they are, according to Beth Mooney. When she became CEO at KeyCorp *and* the first female CEO in the banking industry, she felt a double sense of obligation. "I had this resolve that I have in all things," she says. I thought, 'I'll figure it out because I always do.' And I trade on that instinct—to trust myself."

Karen Parkhill had some apprehension when she began blazing new trails. "There were times when I wished I wasn't the only woman in the room when I was at J. P. Morgan," she says. "Sometimes I felt intimidated. But I learned over time that being the only woman gave me power. It was important for me to understand that and harness it."

"I had this resolve: 'I'll figure it out because I always do.' And I trade on that instinct—to trust myself."

BETH MOONEY

Blazing a new trail often requires a "sixth sense" along with great courage and conviction. Armed with what one of her senior executives refers to as a "corporate crystal ball," E. LaVerne Johnson saw the need to evolve from traditional to virtual classroom learning far ahead of the training industry. Through LaVerne's foresight and ideally timed technology investment—just before 9/11—her company brought learners together from many countries in a virtual environment. She says, "By anticipating a need and responding with a solution for those not wanting to travel just then, we quickly gained a leading industry position in virtual learning, a platform we've expanded significantly over the years."

A positive attitude is another requirement for successful trailblazers. Ilene Lang says, "I've been fired more than once, and that makes it easier to take risks. I think, 'What's the worst that can happen?' I can still have a great line on my résumé and a story to tell about it."

Sometimes you may not have a choice—you need the courage to be a trailblazer because the situation demands nothing less. Denise Morrison says, "If things stray from the status quo, don't wait for everything to get back to normal. Change is the new normal. In fact, it may be riskier *not* to change. And it's so much better to lead change than be a victim of it."

When the trail you're blazing is one that significantly breaks new ground, thinking out of the box is even more important. Lisa Sherman was in on the launch of LogoTV, the first LGBT channel, in 2005. Her team wanted to do something special during the 2008 presidential election, so they invited all the candidates to take part in a televised forum. She says, "We asked all of them to be on 'gay TV,' to talk to a gay audience about gay issues for the first time ever. All of the Democratic candidates agreed to participate, including Barack Obama and Hillary Clinton. We knew in that moment that we were building something really important."

"It's so much better to lead change than be a victim of it."
DENISE MORRISON

Uplifting Future Trailblazers

All new trailblazers need to find their own way, but it helps to study tactics of role models and, maybe more importantly, to just believe that they'll succeed. Others will look to current trailblazers as they start down their own untrodden paths. Even a word or two of encouragement can set a beginner's foot on a new trail. Virginia Albanese says, "It's incumbent upon us as leaders to tell people, 'You can do it. *I know you can.*'"

Every trailblazer makes a difference. But when an *army* of trailblazers emerges at the same time, bigger things happen. Case in point: women in top positions in business. Beth Mooney puts it like this: "Seeing women rise to powerful positions in significant numbers is a phenomenon of our generation. Women have become leaders in meaningful numbers and in virtually every industry and every profession, public and private. There have been women leaders throughout history, but if you consider politics, business, all sorts of different venues, we've really changed the world in a generation."

Two Powerful Words: You Can

For every trailblazer, there are barriers to clear before we can move on. Some may be formidable, and that's when an uplifting voice can help us surmount the biggest obstacles.

Ilene Lang found resistance on the trail she was blazing.

My parents were both college-educated, so there was no question that I would not only go to college, but also to graduate school. This could have been impossible financially except that my great-grandfather, an immigrant watchmaker who worked for a company called Roebuck, died young, and during the Great Depression, my great-grandmother, for sentimental reasons, saved some "worthless pieces of paper"—which turned out to be Sears Roebuck stock certificates. Years later, that money paid for all my schooling plus the down payment on my first house!

So yes, I was lucky as a Jewish girl born in 1943 to be in Chicago, with parents who believed I could succeed at anything. They thought I could be President! I had great encouragement at home. But when I was 11, a religious instructor told me, "You'll never be a leader because you're a girl." And when I got to Harvard, an advisor said, "You're not smart enough to major in math here—in fact, girls aren't smart enough to get As in economics."

But, lucky me, there was always someone else who said, "Try this. Do this. *You can.*"

And, thanks to them, I did.

What, No Pantyhose?

Carla Harris credits the Generation Xers and Millennials with being natural trailblazers and uplifting those around them.

Over the last decade, I've watched women be more authentic in leadership roles—doing things their own way rather than how they'd observed men lead. Not that long ago, women leaders even *dressed* like men, in charcoal gray suits and little paisley ties.

But things changed, beginning with the technology boom of the late '90s. Suddenly, here was an alternative that offered women the same opportunities as Wall Street or consulting—the chance to be intellectually stimulated, have power, and earn a lot of money.

The second change, and the one with greater impact, was the tsunami of Millennials and the Gen Xers who entered the workforce. They had different demands and appetites from the Boomers who were willing to stick to tradition in business. At first, they were a shock to the status quo.

I remember the first time one of my colleagues—who wore charcoal gray suits—noticed the change. She pointed to a young woman investment banker and said, rather horrified, "She's not wearing pantyhose!" At first I thought, "What's the big deal?" And then I remembered. It *was* a big deal for us Boomers because we wouldn't have been caught dead in the office without hose, even in summer! But this was a generation that said, "That makes no sense." And they're right.

This was our first clue that this new generation was going to change how business works, starting with the dress code. As women leaders allow their authenticity to bleed into the corporate environment, the more impact women will have and, in my opinion, the better the companies will do.

Taking a Hard Road

Heather Ettinger had more than one strike against her as she set out on her trailblazing adventure. She was a woman in a mostly male business, and her father was the boss. Clearly, she wasn't received with open arms. But she *did* have a great role model.

I'm a second-generation trailblazer. My dad lost his own father when he was only 12, so it took a lot of courage to start a business on his own. He created an investment firm model that was unique and entrepreneurial. Roulston & Company became recognized nationally and internationally—something I never realized until I worked in Boston and saw the firm from the outside in.

When I was young, my dad wasn't sure if he wanted me to follow his lead or stay in a traditional "woman's" role. But I went to work for him and eventually earned a manager's position...over an all-male team. At first, the men didn't take me seriously, but my dad guided me—with more stick than carrot for a while—so I could make some progress and get the men to respect me. He'd tell me, "Psych them up! Literally shock them!" While others thought he was giving me the easy territories, I chose the toughest ones and turned them around. In the long run, that served me really well. In the short run, however, it wasn't much fun—not only because the territories weren't good, but the clients in those territories didn't like us a whole lot. I had a lot to change there, and I succeeded.

5

Collaboration:
Uplifting Leaders Are Team Players

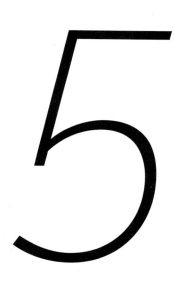

Nobody reaches the top alone, and running a business isn't a one-person job. Our leaders agree that working with people at all levels, inside and outside your company, is essential for success and a great way to uplift others—and themselves. Jenniffer Deckard says, "One person can't ever have all of the best ideas or the best vision or the best way of getting things done." And Barbara Snyder concurs: "All the successful leaders I know and emulate have assembled really talented teams because each one of them has recognized they can't do it alone."

The benefits go beyond just support to get things done. Being included in a collaborative group can change a company's culture, according to Lisa Sherman. She took on the task of redirecting a formerly hierarchical organization into one that values collaboration. As she does this, she says, "I'm driving teamwork, transparency, communications—breaking down old siloes. I've found that people outside of top leadership positions have great ideas, but we need to create an environment for them to more fully participate. While there is often a comfort in being told what to do, most of our employees are looking for the ability to contribute ideas and solutions."

Using Your Personal Style to Uplift Teams

Our leaders emphasize the need to rely on your own style as you collaborate. Karen Parkhill says, "I want people to understand who I am—my philosophies on teamwork, communication, leadership, and continual improvement. What rings true in those philosophies is that no one person is perfect or strong on their own. It takes a team of brave people who are willing to surround themselves with experienced colleagues to create a really good outcome."

Respect is a big part of collaboration, and Sandy Pianalto learned the importance of respect and inclusion the hard way: "We came from Italy, and in Akron, Ohio, there wasn't a lot of diversity then. I watched my parents struggle because people didn't respect them since they couldn't speak English well. So to this day, to every person in every organization I've ever worked with, I always give the utmost respect. People value that, and you know, they will do anything for you." She adds, "Just being humble opens you. People won't be afraid to confide in you, and they'll share thoughts and ideas because they know you'll hear them in a respectful way."

Darla Stuckey knows that it's essential to engage others as you make changes, and collaboration is often the best way to do this. "Sometimes collaboration comes in through the back door," she says. "When you're trying to make a positive change, and if you think you have a good idea that's not being heard, socialize it with a few people. Get some buy-in, and someone else might take it on. It can be better to let others speak for you when you're running into resistance." Collaboration can begin with establishing a healthy mindset for your team. Erika Karp says,

"Figure out a way to let people learn. Let them have a sense that they can achieve their aspirations while still pushing them out of their comfort zone. That's how you build a team. That's creativity. That's innovation."

Without respect from others that comes through collaboration, Karen Parkhill says, you can't be a positive powerful influence: "Power is exemplified in those who can drive change. Change can be influenced from a positive or negative perspective, and those who drive it from a negative perspective do so through sheer force or intimidation. Those who drive it through a positive perspective typically gain the respect of others and motivate them. So first and foremost, you have to earn that respect. Once you have it, use your voice to shed light on issues and offer solutions, whether that's at work or in the community."

For Jackie Woods, authenticity is at the heart of working well together. She says, "It's so important to work hard at building personal one-on-one relationships across your career. Meet people where they are, but never change who *you* are. Someone once said to me, 'You're a chameleon—you don't stand for anything because you're so willing to negotiate and give and take.' That's not true at all. I have core values that *will not be changed*. My approach, my style, my technique—I'm willing to change all that, but not who I am."

Lisa Woll acknowledges that there's no single way to influence and be effective. "You have to figure out how to work with different kinds of stakeholders, different kinds of people," she says. "The question is this: How do you bring most of the people along with you, include them from the beginning, and be sure they feel like they're part of it all? Leadership is really nothing if people aren't with you."

"Bring people along with you, and be sure they feel like they're part of it all. Leadership is really nothing if people aren't with you."
LISA WOLL

Widen the Circle

When you're creating teams, our leaders recommend looking beyond the usual cast of characters. Susan Fuehrer says, "You need to leverage diversity. At my hospital, this means including everyone." Jenniffer Deckard agrees: "The more diversity of thought, experience, perspective, and expertise, the better. It's the same for any group trying to solve, develop, or accomplish something. And that applies from corporate boardrooms to PTAs."

When working with a collaborative group, Lisa Sherman believes it begins with an open, two-way communication style: "I tell people, 'I'd love your help,' and that gets them feeling like they're truly on the team."

Is there a gender difference when it comes to collaboration? Jenniffer Deckard believes that "people differ in their leadership styles, their effectiveness, regardless of gender. To attribute qualities or strengths to gender is a disservice to both sides."

"The more diversity of thought, experience, perspective, and expertise, the better."

JENNIFFER DECKARD

But other leaders point out the differences in collaborative styles. Darla Stuckey says, "In their management approach, male leaders are driven by the bottom line. Some like to appear courageous and confident, even if they don't understand things. But women are more collaborative. They're willing to be questioned, and they consider other people's opinions and needs. Good women leaders aren't scared to ask the tough questions."

Dr. Jerry Sue Thornton believes that women bring more "emotional intelligence" to teams. "We probably delve into the emotional quality of things differently," she says. "Not to say that men don't—and some more than others. Men build teams, but those teams aren't necessarily inclusive. Each team member may be doing his or her own thing toward a team goal. But women are more inclusive in helping each other perform their roles, in helping each other be successful."

Outside the Lines: Working with Other Organizations

Having an established presence in your community can be a huge help when things get rough. Sandy Pianalto tells this story of her experience during the country's financial crisis and Great Recession: "I'd been very active in the community and had a lot of contacts.

I was always willing to listen to different perspectives. So when the economic situation got challenging, I could call business leaders. The country hadn't gone through anything like this in a hundred years—we had no history to go by. Firsthand information from business leaders was very helpful, and because I'd built those relationships *before* the financial crisis, it was much easier to call them and ask them for information on their companies."

Expanding collaboration beyond your own borders can bring benefits for a wider circle of people and enable bigger successes, according to Barbara Snyder, who adds, "Working with other organizations has led to opportunities to do things we could never have done by ourselves."

Power Through Collaboration

Power in business emanates from the ground up and is based on gaining the confidence of the people around you. Sandy Pianalto says:

> For me, power hasn't come through self-confidence and intimidating people, but through the ability to collaborate. People say I'm willing to listen and that I try to get people to work together. When I became chief operating officer, it wasn't because I had the technical skills. It was because the board felt I could help change the culture of the organization and make it more participative. It was because I was willing to work with a lot of different people and get a lot of different viewpoints.

Collaboration Comes from "Team" Work

Two leaders credit a background in sports for their ability to collaborate with diverse teams.

Heather Ettinger says, "There's a common denominator among executives—most of them played competitive sports." She believes sports participation puts people in scenarios where leadership is a big part. "I was never going to be the fastest or the highest scorer, but I was a great passer and played great defense," she says. "It was all about understanding my role on the team."

Jenniffer Deckard believes sports molded her entire approach to life. She says, "I don't think I'd be where I am today without sports. I was raised in a single-parent home, and sports kept me out of trouble. I played four team sports, year-round. My competitive nature drove me to sports, and sports probably enhanced it. I gained confidence." She also recognizes the role of playing sports in her ability to work successfully with others. "Sports gave me self-assurance, but with a team approach. Sports teaches you to *compete as a team*. And I don't think there's any better team sport than volleyball for collaboration, because you don't choose who gets the ball."

Defining a Purpose Together

Denise Morrison shares this uplifting story about how collaboration resulted in an authentic and heartfelt result.

About three years ago, during a time of change, we put together a cross-company/cross-business team—something we'd never done before. We had a really good framework for our strategy, but we hadn't taken the time to define why we were doing this, what was driving us, and what made us different from other food companies. So this team started with the mandate to define our purpose.

Purpose isn't something you make up, like advertising copy. It's something people carry around in their hearts, and articulating it isn't easy. Together, we realized that whenever we said to a consumer, "I work for Campbell's," we'd hear a story about tomato soup and grilled cheese on a cold Friday night, or a Goldfish moment with a child. People would literally break out in stories with happy expressions and love and warmth. So the team came up with this—"Real Food that Matters for Life's Moments"—with the insight that we at Campbell Soup don't make the moments; the *consumer* makes the moments, and we make them a little bit more special.

When you're galvanizing a company that needs to change, you need anchors, and your purpose is one of those anchors. I'm happy that ours was created through collaboration.

6

Advice:
Uplifting Leaders
Share Life Lessons

Life has a funny way of complicating simple things. Business books, courses, lectures, seminars...they usually go into deep descriptions about the profound qualities needed to be a good leader. But when you break it down, the basic requirements are the same ones we learned as children:

> Always be yourself,
> Do the right thing,
> Stay curious,
> Be honest and positive, and
> Trust your inner voice.

The leaders in this book share advice that reaffirms these attributes of being authentic, principled, inquisitive, optimistic, and self-reliant. Their guidance is more specific, of course—and they've proven that it works in their worlds.

"Be who you really are and you'll inspire others to be who they really are. When people can be truly themselves, they'll always excel."

CARLA HARRIS

"Be an open book with close colleagues. If they know something about your personal life, they can more easily understand when you may not be having your best day at work."

KAREN PARKHILL

"When you're making any decision, ask yourself, 'What do I really want to impact and why?' Be thoughtful about your influence, and be authentic."

MARCELLA KANFER ROLNICK

"Bring your whole self to work. I know that's a cliché, but it's been true for me. When I couldn't be fully me and had to hide parts of myself, it limited my creativity and ability to fully engage in the work because it took so much energy to hide."

LISA SHERMAN

THE ORIGINAL YOU

"Trust your own pacing. Know your own limits and don't try to make somebody else's life your life. Decide what's right for you—what's best for you."

JACKIE WOODS

KEEP TRUE TO YOUR VALUES

"I never set out to be a person of success, but rather a person of value with a contribution to make. If you lead with value as a mindset, success will follow."

ANN HARLAN

KEEP TRUE TO YOUR VALUES

"Create your own purpose— follow your passion! Be your passion in your work. Look for a company where you can fully express yourself. Never settle for simply 'a job' just to have a life!"

E. LAVERNE JOHNSON

KEEP TRUE TO YOUR VALUES

"When your personal values line up with your company values, you've found a great place to work. If not, ask yourself if you really want to be there."

ROBIN KILBRIDE

"Early in your career, set a vision. Refresh and align it along the way. But keep refining what you want to be about, what you want your legacy to be."

BETH MOONEY

"Find your own center and stay grounded. It all comes back to being driven to do something in the world that really matters."

MARCELLA KANFER ROLNICK

"Keep your head aligned with your heart. If you can find a job that you feel passionate about, the sky is the limit."

LISA SHERMAN

"Get as many tools in your toolbox as possible. Don't be like a tree with one branch. You want all the branches, so you can be flexible and take on new roles. Know who makes the decision on the next job you want. Engage that person and explain where you want to be."

VIRGINIA ALBANESE

ALWAYS LOOK FOR THINGS TO LEARN

"Remember the basics—communication skills, written and verbal, and persuasive skills. Great leaders are great communicators. It's part of what I believe has made me successful."

ADENA FRIEDMAN

© 2016 Quote from *Uplifting Leaders.*

ALWAYS LOOK FOR THINGS TO LEARN

"Observe and listen. When I first started in business, I was a bit naïve. One of the best things I did was just watch what was going on around me."

BETH MOONEY

© 2016 Quote from *Uplifting Leaders.*

ALWAYS LOOK FOR THINGS TO LEARN

"Take risks. Shake things up. I love this quote: 'A boat that doesn't rock doesn't move.' Don't stay someplace just because it's comfortable or feels safe. Stretch!"

LISA SHERMAN

© 2016 Quote from *Uplifting Leaders.*

ALWAYS LOOK FOR THINGS TO LEARN

"Never be afraid to try something you don't know how to do. When a friend of mine—who went to Harvard Law School and Yale—applied for a job, she told me she didn't think she had all the qualifications. I told her, 'Well, if you had already acquired these skills, why would you want that job? You want a job because it's going to challenge you and allow you to grow professionally and personally."

LISA WOLL

© 2016 Quote from *Uplifting Leaders.*

KEEP AN OPEN PERSPECTIVE

"Be open, but focus on the heart of the matter. Cut through the noise, figure out what's really critical, throw away what's not, and hone in on the important things so you can reach the right conclusions."

ADENA FRIEDMAN

KEEP AN OPEN PERSPECTIVE

"Don't take things too seriously, and have patience. Sometimes I expect everyone to work as hard as I do or be as committed as I am. For other people, there's a whole big life out there."

SUSAN FUEHRER

KEEP AN OPEN PERSPECTIVE

"Find what keeps you steady. For me, the first thing is my faith. The second is my family. And the third is making a difference. I can't do the third thing without keeping the first and second things in mind. If you separate them, you'll find yourself conflicted."

ROBIN KILBRIDE

KEEP AN OPEN PERSPECTIVE

"When things get overwhelming and you feel like you're going down for the count, go deep inside and say, 'I'm going to survive this—I'll do whatever is needed to make a change.' This is where humility comes in, because when somebody else is your boss, they get to set the goals and expectations."

BETH MOONEY

KEEP AN OPEN PERSPECTIVE

"Don't try to balance your life and your career. There's no such thing as balance. Our first tendency is to take time away from ourselves, *but we really need to take a little bit away from* everything *so we're not sacrificing one thing to save another."*

DR. JERRY SUE THORNTON

TRUST YOUR INNER STRENGTH

"Remember that you do have power. *If you're working at what you care about most, it's not power for its own sake. It becomes an awakening—you have this power through your passion, and it can inspire others to make things happen faster and bigger. You have the opportunity to move mountains!"*

JODI BERG

TRUST YOUR INNER STRENGTH

"What you go through makes you who you are. I have more confidence than when I started out, and I've learned to trust the great talent working for me. But leaders have to lead, and you need a clear direction and a clear vision to do that. Then, encourage people to use creativity in how they bring that vision to life."

DENISE MORRISON

TRUST YOUR INNER STRENGTH

"Having self-confidence is half the battle. People want to be around confident people— especially their leaders. I've learned to recognize exactly when my self-confidence is starting to slip, and I figure out a way to get it back."

KAREN PARKHILL

TRUST YOUR INNER STRENGTH

"Learn the power in patience. Usually good things come if you are passionate about what you do and just wait."

DARLA STUCKEY

TRUST YOUR INNER STRENGTH

"Be willing to work harder than anybody else, to roll up your sleeves when others have said, 'Okay, this is enough.' You can't get away from hard work or 'time on task' if you really want to get to the top of your field."

DR. JERRY SUE THORNTON

TRUST YOUR INNER STRENGTH

"In the middle of a massive to-do list, step back and ask yourself, 'How am I leading?' 'What can I do better?' and 'Where are the opportunities that I'm missing?'"

LISA WOLL

TRUST YOUR INNER STRENGTH

"Be aggressive in your ideas, but not your demeanor. You want people to really hear what you're saying, not react to how you're saying it."

DENISE MORRISON

UPLIFTING IS A UNIVERSAL GOAL

"Remembering the bigger picture is essential. My mantra is 'Success is not forever, and failure is not fatal.'"

DR. JERRY SUE THORNTON

UPLIFTING IS A UNIVERSAL GOAL

"When I was very ill, I learned that every single day is a blessing. I wanted my time here to matter—that there's a reason why I was on the planet. And that's what drives me. I've been using every day since as a gift and an opportunity. I ask myself, 'What impact did I have today?' 'Whose lives did I touch?'"

JODI BERG

UPLIFTING IS A UNIVERSAL GOAL

"This is the advice I'd give to my 20-year-old self: Realize that every change, every twist, every turn leads to the next thing and ultimately to exactly where you're supposed to be."

LISA SHERMAN

MY FAVORITE QUOTE:

....

....

....

....

....

....

Pass It On: The Power of Inspiration

It's important to remember that no matter how mundane our work may seem, it affects people's lives. Jodi Berg tells this uplifting story that reminds us that we're all more than cogs in a business machine.

> One of my employees gave me a wonderful example that illustrates how knowing your purpose makes a huge difference in your work. Carmen worked on our production line, building machines that help nourish people, including those who can't eat normally. She read a testimonial from a mother whose daughter needed to be tube-fed. Our Vitamix machine made it possible for that little girl to switch from processed food to whole foods, which made a significant impact on her health. When Carmen read that letter, she was overcome with emotion and joy. She said to me, 'My hands may have built the machine that saved a little girl's life. I will never again build a machine without thinking about that.' Carmen has since been promoted and is helping others connect to their purpose.

Know Where You're Going—a Personal Mission

Most business leaders have helped write their organizations' mission statements—probably more than once. Denise Morrison recommends writing one for yourself.

> I was impressed with the chapter on personal missions in Stephen Covey's *7 Habits of Highly Effective People*. I asked myself a tough question: "If I don't know what I stand for as a leader, how can I expect anyone to follow me?"

> So I set out to write that mission. This required locking myself in a room and refusing to come out until I had one I could be proud of. I did a lot of soul-searching. I thought about power as giving, about leadership as service.

> When I was done, this was my statement: "My mission is to serve as a leader, live a balanced life, and apply ethical principles to make a significant difference."

> By a "balanced life," I didn't mean work/life balance. I meant the balance of spiritual, academic, and physical. When those three circles are in balance, then I'm at my personal best. If one of them gets *out* of balance, I work to get it back *in* balance to be at my best performance."

Denise and many other leaders rely on a personal mission to guide them through daily challenges on the job and in life. They all agree it's worth the effort

"Be Prepared" Isn't Just for Girl Scouts

Beth Mooney stresses the importance of preparation and staying present in any career, right from the start.

When you get the top spot, you're the dog who chased the car and caught it. I remember how I felt when that happened to me. Even though I had aspired to a position like this my whole life, I was in stark terror mode. In my fear, I wondered if I'd ever be able to say this was the most satisfying time in my career.

But I had a deep sense of obligation, and I knew people were watching my every move. So from my first day, with purposeful consciousness, I began planning how I would reach out to people and map out the goals that I set. I was determined to come to work every day prepared and organized with a thoughtful plan.

How you show up every day is incredibly important. When you go into meetings or have an opportunity to address employees or a community group, be prepared. Everything you do needs to be conscious. It needs to be purposeful. You can never sleepwalk through your day.

Influencing Change by Being Your Honest Self

Lisa Sherman prompted significant change at a company by refusing to compromise her authenticity.

In 1995, the CEO of my company put everybody through diversity training. I was in a group with my peers and all our senior and executive vice presidents. The facilitator had set up easel boards with statements like "Black people are..." and "Hispanics are..." and "Gay people are..." We were asked to be candid about our biases and write them on the boards.

At this point, I had not come out at work. I was out in every other part of my life, but I was worried that my being gay would somehow hurt my career even though I had been at that company for some time.

Everybody in this session knew there were representatives of most of these groups in the room, but nobody knew about me. So they wrote things like "Black people are good dancers" and "Hispanics are family-oriented." I still get chills when I remember what was written on the "Gay people are..." easel. The comments said, "Gay people are sick." "Gay people spread disease." "Gay people are trying to convert our children." I looked around the room and thought, "Who wrote these things?" I knew in that moment that I could no longer stay there. I resigned.

On my last day, I went to the CEO's office to say goodbye. I had the courage then to tell him why I was leaving. He was blown away. He'd had no idea about me. I explained that I couldn't work in a place where domestic partnership benefits had been blocked over and over and where it took two years to write the words "sexual orientation" into the diversity policy.

I got a new job, and after I'd been there a while, a friend from my former workplace told me that the board had once more been discussing domestic partnership benefits, and when it looked like they'd be blocked yet again, my former CEO stood up and told them my story. He said, "When Lisa left and told me why, I wasn't sure I believed her, but sitting here listening to all of you, I see she was right. Find a way to have domestic partnership benefits in place as soon as possible." And within six months, it was done.

7

Transformers:
Uplifting Leaders
Leave Legacies

As great leaders blaze trails, they leave footprints. They change the landscape in big or small ways, but they make differences. They begin with grand goals and may achieve many of them, or they may change things in ways they didn't intend to. But there's no doubt that they leave their personal touch. We asked our leaders how they view and use their power to transform their organizations or create an environment to help people grow. There's an element of "uplifting" in each one.

Transforming a Business

E. LaVerne Johnson has tried to encourage her people to "wake up each morning with a passion for coming to work." She takes it a step further, by getting them to their "level of incompetence" as quickly as possible. "That causes them to feel challenged," she says, "and then their adrenalin begins to flow. They're awake and they have a bit of welcome 'fear of the unknown.' This kind of environment engages them in learning and reaching to meet their goals. It's also a catalyst in retaining employees. Who doesn't want to be 'stretched' every day?"

"Who doesn't want to be 'stretched' every day?"

E. LAVERNE JOHNSON

Uplifting leaders transform their workplaces through servant leadership. The term is likely no better represented than at the Louis Stokes Cleveland VA Medical Center, with both the employees and veterans. Susan Fuehrer has always seen her role in this light: "We wouldn't be here if not for these veterans who were willing to lay their lives on the line for us. I've always been here for my staff and our vets through thick and thin, and our results are world-class."

Leaders with a heart want employees to know the value they contribute. Darla Stuckey says, "I've always wanted everyone to feel that what they're doing is important. If they don't understand the larger context, they can't see that. But when they do, they become a passionate, engaged, empowered workforce and make appropriate decisions. My role has always been to support them, to show that I have confidence in them."

Barbara Snyder believes in the power of trust. She says, "I've seen my number-one job as building trust—or rebuilding it. Everything else comes from that. In the academic setting, it's important in both internal and external communities, so people know that if we say we're going to do something, we do it. Everybody wants to know that when you give your word, it's valuable."

"I've always wanted everyone to feel that what they are doing is important."

DARLA STUCKEY

Where Transformation Begins

In business, transformation needs someone (or better yet, many people) to drive it. Marcella Kanfer Rolnick played a key role in championing sustainability at her company but was not alone in doing so. "There are many great people at GOJO who are helping to connect sustainability to our company's purpose, "Saving Lives and Making Life Better through Well-Being Solutions." Our purpose, which we made explicit in the mid-1990s, has created a North Star and a shared understanding of why we're all here. And it certainly attracts, motivates, aligns, and retains people. When we declared our purpose, we realized that we were not just a chemical company or even a soap company—we were more than that. We were bringing *health and wellness* to people. Transforming our self-concept in this way has had a great influence on our culture and how we think about our role in the world."

When transformation is at the heart of a business, driving change for the company has to be genuine. Dr. Jean Rogers has had this as one of her goals. She says, "Change needs to come from a place of authenticity and from caring about issues personally. Without authenticity, it's very difficult to have the fortitude, the staying power, and the believability to make it happen."

Ilene Lang was hired to create a transformation. "I didn't learn that until after I got the job. I found out that the person who led the search told the Catalyst board of directors, 'If you want change, you want Ilene. If you *don't* want change, you *don't* want Ilene.' In my new leadership position, I worked to preserve the best because I believe in building from where you are, always looking for the strengths and building on the positive."

Once a desired transformation is complete, the adventures continue. Jenniffer Deckard says, "I never see myself as having arrived at something great. I always feel like I'm on the journey.

I'm asking, 'What's my next step?' I don't mean the next upward movement, but the next thing I need to be doing to make an impact somewhere."

Transformation Requires Power

"Power" is an elusive term. It's not a course you take in business school. But according to our leaders, those who rise to the C-Suite have to learn what power really is, how to handle it, and how to use it for positive transformation. But what constitutes "power"? Carla Harris defines power as "the ability to get things done, either by your own hand or by influencing others to exert the energy to get it done." Lisa Woll says, "Power is the ability to make things happen, getting the right people together. It's the ability to convene, act, and influence."

There's a big difference between *earned* power and *entitled* power. Erika Karp states, "Power derived through buy-in is much, much greater than power that's assumed and entitled. There's a big difference between authority and responsibility and power. And there's a big difference between the extent to which influence and power are legitimately granted versus assumed, entitled, and taken."

Once you have power, our leaders say, you need to learn how to use it correctly. Susan Fuehrer says, "I rarely use the word *power*. I'd call it 'respected influence to make improvements.' In my journey, I started at the very bottom. I learned that if you have a title or a salary, you have power to get things done. The title itself didn't necessarily matter. What matters was that you had a good idea and you could, for the right reason, sell that idea to others."

Robin Kilbride has a similar view. "From what I've observed, I think the best way to use power is to help others be successful, to find opportunities and give people a chance to work on them, asking questions and helping them think things through so they can succeed."

Ann Harlan believes that real power should always be exercised with humility and empathy—and with a certain amount of fearlessness and risk-taking, "When I was first starting out, there were not many women at the larger law firms, much less in the legal departments of large companies, and we had to strategically pick our battles. Once we established ourselves as team players and showed that we could make the tough decisions, it was possible to have a voice for change and to effectively use that voice for change. The same holds true today. Focusing on and really sensing others' emotions and understanding what causes people to take certain positions allows me to appreciate different perspectives and to exercise influence from a place of empathy and greater understanding. For me, leading from a place of understanding is a more meaningful and more effective approach."

But power has requirements. Erika Karp says, "There is another piece of the power puzzle—when you're making decisions that require responsibility, there has to be accountability and autonomy. Otherwise, it's problematic from the standpoint of execution."

So how do you *get* power? Lisa Woll says, "Sometimes you're given a position that *presumes* power, but you can also *assume* power through influence and people's perception of you." Robin Kilbride adds, "Before I had actual power, I had a *voice*. I was invited to share my opinion. It really didn't matter if I was the boss or not. And I think people sometimes miss opportunities to learn and contribute because they're too concerned about whether they have authority."

Legacies: Uplifting Through Transformation

When most people leave a job or retire, a few colleagues remember them for their best (or worst) traits. But when a *leader* moves on, they hope to leave a deeper, wider, more lasting impression. We asked our leaders, "What do you want to be remembered for?" All of their answers are transformative.

EXPANDING POSSIBILITIES

We all hope to make a mark on the world, but leaders have the chance to really touch people's lives and make big differences. Ann Harlan says, "I like to quote Lewis Carroll as I think of the legacy I wish to leave: *One of the deep secrets of life is that all that is really worth the doing is what we do for others.* What's important is thinking about the people, professionally and personally, who are part of your world and asking, 'What will we do together and what will I do for them that will make a difference and make us all better?' For me, it does hold true that doing good almost always results in doing well. At the very least, it makes the journey more rewarding."

Lisa Sherman says, "My organization has a legacy of driving important social change that precedes me by seven decades, and I believe it will continue that important work long after I'm gone. I hope I have contributed to that enduring legacy and in some small way to inspire change and improve lives." Robin Kilbride says, "Leaving my company a better place is the biggest responsibility I have. And that means that our people feel challenged and know they can contribute."

Dr. Jerry Sue Thornton wants to be remembered as "one who helped make a difference in many people's lives—and together with others, helped make the world a better place."

RAISING PEOPLE TO NEW HEIGHTS

One of the most powerful gifts a leader can give her people is helping them advance and grow. Carla Harris says, "I'd like people to remember that I positively impacted a lot of careers." Virginia Albanese says, "I ran a successful business with people in mind, in a nice way, with a really engaged workforce, and I wanted all of us to win." Marcella Kanfer Rolnick hopes to be remembered as "helping our culture be ever better at making a space for people to both stand up and step back—and to know the difference, making it easy for our colleagues everywhere throughout the organization to bring their full selves and personal integrity to the company."

Preparing young people for the future is the legacy Sandy Pianalto wants to leave. She says, "I have a real passion for education, and now that I'm retired, I'd like my legacy to be about the importance of education. We've got to figure out the formula for making sure our young people have the skills necessary to not only participate but to thrive in today's global economy." E. Laverne Johnson says, "Retirement has no appeal whatsoever to me. I plan to die at my desk or on the golf course! So my legacy, I hope, will be the young people I have brought in—quite a few of whom have grown older along with me—and they have been inspired to achieve great accomplishments and the betterment of the world."

Women are at the center of the legacy Heather Ettinger wants to leave. She says, "I've tried to help all my peers succeed, to be sure all voices were heard, and to empower all our clients. I also worked to empower women. They are the agents of social change and bring everybody along." Karen Parkhill agrees: "Because I spent my entire career in male-dominated companies, I've tried to inspire other women to stick with it, to ultimately achieve that better balance. I know that the world, our companies, and our communities will be much better off when we have greater gender balance."

STRENGTHENING THE BUSINESS

Clearly, every leader strives to advance the companies they serve. As corporate executives, several of our leaders want to be remembered for the way their businesses fared during their tenure. Beth Mooney says, "I was the first female CEO of a top-20 U.S. bank, but I hope that will be a footnote, not a headline. We were a company that helped make *all* women and diverse people in leadership roles footnotes, not headlines. I'd like people to remember that, in my tenure, investors were rewarded, employees felt valued and thrived working here, we were successful for our communities and our clients, and we were a good corporate citizen." Darla Stuckey wants to "leave our Society better than how I found it—a stronger place financially—and to elevate people in my profession. I want the corporate secretary role to be known and understood, and I want these individuals to be revered and respected." Jenniffer Deckard says, "I hope to leave a legacy of serving others, but also be remembered as a strong leader."

> *"I was the first female CEO of a top-20 U.S. bank, but I hope that will be a footnote, not a headline."*
>
> **BETH MOONEY**

Effecting positive change was another theme in our leaders' legacies. Dr. Jean Rogers says, "I truly hope my legacy is one of systemic change in the information available to the capital markets to drive trillions of dollars of income to more sustainable outcomes, and for the markets to understand the true environmental and social impacts of investing." Erika Karp says, "I worked to bring more honor to the capital markets and helped people learn how to leverage the tools of capitalism to facilitate global prosperity." Lisa Woll wants people to know that "in all the different areas where I've worked, I've been effective in helping to change a paradigm, to create strategies to more effectively advance a range of issues. I also tried to help other people become more effective and to deepen their own commitments."

PASSING ON THE PASSION

There's a kind of transcendent legacy many leaders wish to leave, with authenticity and positivity at its heart. Jodi Berg wants to be remembered for "caring deeply, living fully, and stewarding the opportunities and lives that God has put into my life. I may not be remembered personally, but knowing that I have given people wings to take flight and make the world a better place in their own way will lift my soul for eternity."

Ilene Lang wants to be remembered as "a change-maker and a glass-breaker. I had successes and I had failures, and I learned from them." Susan Fuehrer says, "I always tried to do the right thing, I listened with my head and my heart, and I never compromised my values. I was transparent and open." The legacy of Denise Morrison strikes the same chord: "I was authentic, and I had the courage of my convictions. I never asked people to do anything I wasn't willing to do myself. My passion has been and will be the future of real food and helping people live better lives."

In the end, most leaders echoed the sentiments of Barbara Snyder: "The ultimate compliment is that things were a lot better when a leader left than the day she arrived. If people say that about me, I'll be happy."

Some legacies have yet to be written. Adena Friedman admits, "I don't think I've accomplished enough to be able to answer that question yet."

Margaret Wong says, "Once, I would have liked my tombstone to say, 'The best immigration lawyer in the world who beat all other immigration lawyers.' But now I feel differently. Honestly, I'm still figuring out what I'd like my legacy to be!"

Jackie Woods adds, "I don't want to leave a legacy yet. I want to keep going! But when I do have one, I'd like it to be personal. Like this: My granddaughter was really excited to come for a visit, and when her father asked her why, she said, "Because she's always so happy to see me. Now, that's a legacy."

A New Kind of Family: Sharing the Inspiration

Each of us who has benefitted from someone else's inspiration feels a sense of responsibility to pass on that gift. A lesson we've learned the hard way may ease someone else's burden or help them avoid pain. And while we're doing that, the inspiration keeps flowing both ways.

Denise Morrison has been uplifting a group of younger women for the past three years and getting inspiration in return.

> I was looking for a way to pass on leadership stories and introduce our Millennials to some Campbell's executives as role models. I had another reason for creating this group of young women—I wanted to learn about *them*. I know they shop differently and eat differently and socialize with food differently from their parents. I wanted this to be a "give and get"—I give you leadership coaching, you tell me what your world is like.

> It's been very interesting on a number of fronts. First, they love the "art of conversation"! These are people who text all the time—they don't *talk*. So sitting around a table, sharing a meal and talking about leadership has been really energizing. It's been powerful for me because I'm giving them what I know, but at the same time, they're uplifting *me*.

The Hourglass Imperative

Sometimes a visual aid can help us remember how today's work can contribute to transforming the future. Jenniffer Deckard tells this story:

> When I took over the role of president, I held a leadership meeting and gave everybody an hourglass. The inscription read: "How are we going to spend our time?"

> Our challenge was to spend our time building something for the next generation, to make sure they had opportunities just as we had been given opportunities, and to serve our Fairmount family, our customers, and our community. This inspiration served us well and kept us focused on the significant legacy to which care we had been entrusted and to continued improvement for the benefit of everyone.

An Uplifting Legacy of Spirit

Ilene Lang talks about two kinds of legacies:

Some people advise that you should think about your legacy when you *start* a job—not when you're leaving it. I've been thinking about my legacy for a long time.

A great example of someone who left a lasting legacy was Martha Graham, the pioneer of modern dance. More than 90 years ago, she invented this new form of artistic expression. She created ballets and invited composers to write music designed to showcase her choreography. She founded the first integrated dance company. When she died in 1991, she left a huge amount of intellectual property as her legacy—what I call the "Martha Museum." But she left so much more.

The second part of her legacy was the "Martha Spirit"—her force for innovation. She was about change. She was about empowering young people to dance and inviting young composers to create music. Of the two legacies, that's the one that is most lasting and valuable. Her spirit keeps people pushing the envelope, exploring, moving things. So it's a *living* legacy.

When I retired, an announcement posted on our intranet was the most meaningful tribute I received. The post included events that happened during my tenure, but it concluded like this: "It's not Ilene's effectiveness we'll miss the most. It's her inspirational leadership, her unwavering commitment to our mission, and her incredible personal warmth."

The company honored me by establishing the Lang Legacy Fund. The money contributed will continue the causes I was most passionate about—advancing women of color, inclusive leadership training, and engaging men as partners in gender equality.

To me, a legacy isn't about building monuments. It's not about a Martha Museum. It's what you've accomplished with a Martha Spirit.

The Power of Music

Often, transformers transform themselves. Carla Harris is also an author and recording artist. She has found that inspiration and transformation enhance each other—both in the business world and, for her, in music.

I've been singing since I was nine, and really avidly in church choirs since I was 12 or 13. I always thought that someday, I'd record *something*, but I didn't realize how much I would love recording gospel music. Gospel music is so uplifting. It really doesn't matter which denomination you are—when you hear music that's so full of hope and joy and someone sings it well, it can make you feel good! All that's going on in the world can bring you down, make you sad, make you pause, even paralyze you. But this is something that can make you think differently, even for a few moments.

The first time I stepped onstage to sing at Carnegie Hall, I told myself that I wasn't going to leave the same person I was when I'd walked through the door. And that's what has transpired each time I've performed there.

Conclusion

Heeding advice from the late Mary Griffith (our former boss, mentor, and friend to whom we dedicated this book), we continually "do the things we don't know how to do to learn how to do them"—such as publishing this book. The same holds true for the women we interviewed. No one gave them step-by-step directions to successfully advance in their careers. They learned as they took the roads less traveled, tackling challenges and pursuing opportunities along the way. They persevered, leaving lasting footprints and lifelong lessons for others.

Gathering our leaders' stories and lessons provided the two of us an opportunity not only to spend time together (which we often don't get to do), but prompted us to ask: What positive footprints—uplifting lessons—can we leave for others? In what ways can we pay it forward by sharing advice from our experiences over the years?

Reflecting on these thought-provoking questions, and keeping in mind we are celebrating our 20th year together in business, we share our list of 20 memorable quotes and lessons. While we admit our "Top 20" list does not consist of all unique or original thoughts, we know these lessons strengthened our character and resolve to succeed. They remain constant reminders of those who uplifted us—or pushed us to lift ourselves by our own bootstraps—to grow and learn.

BY BARB BROWN AND MARGIE FLYNN

1. "Remember the power of 'thank you' and a smile."

2. "Treasure those around you, and when it feels right, go ahead and give them a hug!"

3. "Before you judge, consider what it's like to step into the realm of someone else's experience."

4. "Don't take yourself too seriously."

5. "There's no such thing as a dumb question."

6. "What goes around comes around."

7. "Take time to celebrate."

8. "When you find your passion at work, it no longer feels like working at all."

9. "The truth is, there is no such thing as work/life balance, but it remains a pursuit worth fighting for!"

10. "Failure is not the worst thing that can happen. Not trying is."

11. "Perspective is everything."

12. "Ask for help when people still have the opportunity to do so."

13. "While you've got the reins, know when to hold the rope tight, and more important, when to let it loose."

14. "Make time for others without expecting anything in return."

15. "Believe in yourself and others will believe in you."

16. "Take time for yourself. Work will go on without you."

17. "A healthy dose of pessimism is an optimist's best friend."

18. "Never forget your roots; they keep you grounded."

19. "Everything happens for a reason. Believe in fate and faith."

20. "Embrace your failures as much as your successes."

You too have an opportunity to leave lasting footprints—lessons to uplift others. What are your "Top 20"? And how will you pay it forward by sharing your lessons with others? Pause. Write. Share. #UpliftingLeaders

Acknowledgments

We extend our sincere appreciation to all who helped make this book a reality. Through your valued support, encouragement, and commitment, we fulfilled a dream of publishing a book that we hope inspires others while giving back to young, underprivileged women who wish to further their education. Thanks to all of you for being part of BrownFlynn's 20-year anniversary commemorative project!

....

Veronica Hughes (our dedicated, uplifting editor)

All the amazing leaders featured in this book, and especially:

- Beth Mooney (our champion and author of our Foreword)

Our entire BrownFlynn team, and most notably:

- Jennifer Griffith (book designer)
- Drew Auld (supporting designer)
- Marissa Brydle
- Julianne Potter
- Kate Lasco

Others who were instrumental in facilitating key interviews and/or providing support along the way:

- Kristin Andress, CEO, Andress Consulting
- Scott Beckerman, Senior Vice President & Director of Corporate Sustainability, Comerica
- Trina Evans, Executive Vice President and Director of Corporate Center, KeyCorp
- Evan Harvey, Director of Corporate Responsibility, Nasdaq

- David Hill, Senior Communications Specialist, FedEx Custom Critical
- Chuck Fowler, Director & Chair of the Executive Committee, Fairmount Santrol, and Chairman of the Board of Trustees, Case Western Reserve University
- Shar Olivier, Director of Sustainability and CSR, and Global Business Developer, International Institute for Learning
- Dave Stangis, Vice President, Corporate Social Responsibility and Sustainability, Campbell Soup Company

Consolidated Solutions, Cleveland, OH (book printer)

YWCA Greater Cleveland Team

- Margaret Mitchell
- Rebecca Calkin

Mansour Gavin (for our trademark search)

Those who kindly provided testimonials of our book (see back cover)

We also wish to acknowledge the many wonderful mentors who uplifted us over the years, some of whom deserve special recognition. Your invaluable lessons and profound advice will remain with us forever.

Because we have been so fortunate to work side-by-side for nearly 27 years, we have many mentors in common. Our BrownFlynn advisors over the years, including Bill Conway, Chuck Fowler, Randy McShepard, Paul Clark, Leslie Dunn, Polly Clemo, and Mike McPhillips. Our mentors from National City who believed in us during our years there, including Ed Brandon, Bill Robertson, Vince DiGirolamo, Bill MacDonald and Tom Richlovsky. And those who have humbly shared servant leadership lessons—Joe Williams and Albert Ratner. Thanks to all of you and to the many others we may have forgotten.

FROM BARB

I would like to thank my many role models throughout my life, beginning with my Mom and Dad, the late Monica and Bill O'Brien. My aunt, Roseanne O'Brien, who was my first example of a class-act professional woman I can remember. My teachers and professors who gave me confidence that I carry with me today, including Ann Carr, my second-grade teacher, and Dr. Jackie Schmidt and Dr. Joe Miller of John Carroll University. There are others whom I have lost touch with but remain in my heart. Pam Sus, who helped me get my first "real" job at Crest Communications, and Bob Vorel, Crest's founder. Larry Rosenthal, a former executive at Cardinal Industries in Columbus who hired me after I had been fired from a job that wasn't a good fit for me or my employer. And thanks to Robin Lawrie, my boss at Cardinal, who taught me how to become a great editor.

Finally, and most important, I am forever grateful for my best friend and business partner, Margie Flynn, from meeting her on my first double date with my soon-to-be husband, to her calling me several years later wondering if I would be interested in a part-time job at National City, to being by my side at BrownFlynn for the past 20 years. The vast majority of credit for this book belongs to Margie—thank you for allowing me to be on this phenomenal journey with you! Hugs!

FROM MARGIE

With tremendous gratitude, I acknowledge all those who taught, inspired, supported, trusted, guided, and even chided me over the years. Each of you influenced my life in defining ways and uplifted me at times when I needed it most. Beginning with my parents—the late Joe and Mary Pigott—who ran a tight household ship (including a "Family Council") while setting positive examples through their hard work, loving care, and dedication to raising five independent, determined children. I wish to specially acknowledge my father ("Big Joe") for the leadership lessons and commitment to community instilled in me and which continue to be instilled in others through his legacy.

My parents also ensured we were blessed with great educations, with one teacher standing above all others in my formative years—Sister Ann Letitia, who taught me in first grade. Her gracious smile, constant encouragement, and patience when I talked too much will never be forgotten. I also will be forever indebted to Ned Grossman, who passed on numerous lessons at my first "real" job out of college—most notably, the importance of building lasting relationships, and the power of two simple words: "thank you." Additionally, I have learned valuable life lessons from each of my siblings, including my late brother Mike Pigott's advice and support when Barb and I opened our firm as well as the many positive examples he imparted to others upon his death. And to those who have shared countless leadership lessons with great care and compassion—Denise Reading, David Plate, and Chris Ronayne, to name a few.

Lastly, there are no words to fully express my thanks to Barb Brown, my "BFF," incredible mentor, and business partner. Her entrepreneurial spirit, visionary thinking, and calculated risk-taking never wanes—as it was Barb who planted the idea to launch our firm and stood at my side through thick and thin. She uplifts me every day through her leadership, inspiration, genuineness, laughter, mixed-up idioms (also a trait of mine), and warm hugs. I'm truly honored to write this first book together, and I'm sure others will follow. Hugs and here's to ya, "Babs"!

About the Authors

Since founding BrownFlynn, Barb Brown and Margie Flynn have embodied tenacity, resilience, passion, and integrity. They capitalized on their drive and complementary strengths to build a business focused on "doing well by doing good." They are true pioneers. From 1990 to 1995, they were one of the first job-sharing partners in corporate America. While promoted and supported by most of executive management, a new Chairman/CEO was selected...and out with the job share. Not to be dissuaded, the two continued pioneering and became entrepreneurs. By signing a sizeable contract with their former employer, they each invested a mere $500 and launched BrownFlynn in January 1996.

Under Barb's and Margie's leadership, BrownFlynn began as generalists, providing strategic change management communications services to Northeast Ohio companies. In 1998, they challenged themselves to market toward their passion—helping companies embrace strategic community relationships while delivering a tangible return on investment. Dubbing themselves a "community relationship management" consulting firm, the company advised clients on strategic philanthropy, employee volunteerism, non-profit partnerships, and signature programs—all while communicating clients' efforts to improve their reputation, engage their employees, and develop partnerships to enhance their license to operate.

Wanting to measure the value of their work, BrownFlynn began utilizing an international standard for corporate responsibility reporting, the Global Reporting Initiative (GRI). During this same time, the term "corporate citizenship" took on more meaning—not just philanthropy, but social and environmental responsibility, or "sustainability." Some corporations were skeptical about the financial benefit of being environmentally and socially responsible. However, in 2009, recognizing a need and opportunity to educate the corporate sector on sustainability's financial benefits, BrownFlynn became the first U.S.-certified training partner for GRI.

Since that time, Barb and Margie have evolved the company further as a corporate sustainability and governance consulting firm serving global and national clients. The company has been actively involved in numerous sustainability initiatives, including serving as an inaugural Advisory Partner to the Sustainability Accounting Standards Board, the only U.S. consultancy partner to Ecovadis (a global leader in sustainable supply chain assessments), and a founding member of the U.S. Business Council for Sustainable Development. In addition, BrownFlynn established a strategic partnership with Sustainserv, a Zurich- and Boston-based sustainability consulting firm, to expand its global reach and provide a wider array of services to its clients.

BrownFlynn's transformation demonstrates Barb's and Margie's drive to innovate and ability to provide creative solutions for clients. Never satisfied with the status quo, they and their tremendously capable team seek to expand and diversify their business by listening to clients, following global trends, speaking at national conferences, and identifying differentiation opportunities. And, every step of the way, they never lose sight of their firm's vision—to create a world where all companies operate in a manner that enables current and future generations to thrive.

More About Our Interviewees

VIRGINIA ALBANESE
President and Chief Executive Officer, FedEx Custom Critical

Virginia Albanese is president and chief executive officer of FedEx Custom Critical. She began her career at FedEx Custom Critical in 1986 and quickly worked her way up the ranks, serving in several senior level roles before being named president and CEO. In 2013 she was appointed by Ohio Governor John Kasich to the Kent State Board of Trustees, and is past chair of The Boys and Girls Club of the Western Reserve and the Greater Akron Chamber of Commerce. Virginia currently serves on the boards of directors of Akron Children's Hospital and the Akron Community Foundation. She has been recognized for her leadership roles both professionally and in the community, and was recently inducted into the Northeastern Ohio Business Hall of Fame. Virginia has received the Leadership Excellence Award from the National Diversity Council (2014), and has been named to the Inside Business Power 100 list for five years straight.

JODI L. BERG
President and Chief Executive Officer, Vitamix Corporation

Jodi Berg is fourth-generation president and chief executive officer of Vitamix Corporation (Vitamix), a family-owned manufacturer recognized as the world leader in high-performance blenders for the consumer and commercial foodservice markets. After a successful career in the hospitality industry, she joined Vitamix with a directive to lead its overseas expansion. The company's products, designed and assembled in Northeast Ohio, are now available in more than 140 countries around the world, and the organization received the nation's highest export recognition—the President's "E Star" Award—in 2014. She also led Vitamix's household and commercial divisions before becoming president and chief executive officer. Under her leadership, Vitamix revenue has grown by more than 300 percent, and the number of employees and sales representatives has more than tripled. She won the EY National Entrepreneur of the Year Award in the Family Business category for creating a global brand, transforming the organizational structure of the company, and leading the creation and implementation of a value-based and laser-focused culture.

JENNIFFER D. DECKARD
President and Chief Executive Officer, Fairmount Santrol

Jenniffer Deckard joined Fairmount Santrol (then Fairmount Minerals) in 1994 and was soon named chief financial officer, serving until 2011 when she was named president and subsequently chief executive officer in 2013. In October 2014, Jenniffer and the company's leadership team led Fairmount Santrol to its initial public offering and the company is now traded on the New York Stock Exchange (FMSA). Jenniffer has been recognized by *Crain's Cleveland Business* in its annual "Forty Under 40" list, and she was named the 2008 "CFO of the Year" for large privately held businesses in Greater Cleveland. She currently serves on the Weatherhead School of Management's Visiting Committee for Case Western Reserve University, and actively serves on the advisory boards of the Cleveland Foundation and RPM International Inc. The Deckard family is actively engaged in multiple educational and civic programs and have both opened their home and provided resources to help serve children within the Geauga County and Greater Cleveland Foster Care System.

HEATHER ETTINGER
Managing Partner, Fairport Asset Management

As managing partner of Fairport Asset Management, Heather specializes in helping clients and their families create financial plans to guide them through life transitions. Heather has devoted more than 25 years to the financial services industry and has held several leadership roles at the company and on the numerous boards for which she has served. In 2015 Heather was recognized on *InvestmentNews'* inaugural "Women to Watch" list for her lasting impact on the financial industry, and she was named to the "Top 50 Distinguished Women in Wealth Management" by *Wealth Management* magazine in 2008. Heather has co-authored two studies about women and their unique needs and has been featured in many publications, including the *Wall Street Journal, InvestmentNews, Barrons,* and *Bloomberg.* She serves on the board of directors of University Hospitals, The Private Trust Company, and Asurint-One Source Technology.

ADENA FRIEDMAN
President and Incoming Chief Executive Officer, Nasdaq

Adena Friedman, currently President and Chief Operating Officer, on January 1, 2017, will assume the role of Chief Executive Officer of Nasdaq, the company that created the world's first electronic stock market and today provides trading, clearing, exchange technology, listing, information and public company services across six continents. Nasdaq's technology powers more than 70 marketplaces in 50 countries and 1 in 10 of the world's securities transactions. It is home to more than 3,700 listed companies with a market value of $10.0 trillion and has approximately 18,000 corporate clients. Ms. Friedman rejoined Nasdaq in 2014 as President, after serving as Chief Financial Officer and Managing Director of The Carlyle Group from March 2011 to June 2014. Before Carlyle, Ms. Friedman was a key member of Nasdaq's management team for over a decade, serving in a variety of roles including head of the company's data products business, head of corporate strategy, as well its Chief Financial Officer. Ms. Friedman is credited with significant contributions to the strategy and expansion of the organization, helping to create one of the most diversified exchanges in the world today. She played an instrumental role in the company's acquisition strategy, overseeing the acquisitions of INET, OMX, and the Philadelphia and Boston Exchanges. She originally joined Nasdaq in 1993.

SUSAN M. FUEHRER
Medical Center Director, Louis Stokes Cleveland VA Medical Center

Susan Fuehrer was appointed the medical center director for the Louis Stokes Cleveland VA Medical Center (VAMC) in 2010 after beginning her career there several decades prior. She joined the Cleveland VAMC as a management intern, held several positions over the years, and was serving as associate director before her appointment to medical center director. The Cleveland VAMC is the third-largest VA in the country, and Susan oversees the care of 115,000 veterans across Northeast Ohio. Susan currently serves on the boards of directors for Cleveland's Healthcare Information Management Executives, the Northeast Ohio Chapter of the American Red Cross, the Center for Health Affairs, and the Cuyahoga Community College Foundation, and is the past chairman of the Cleveland Federal Executive Board.

M. ANN HARLAN
Co-CEO, Harlan Peterson Partners, LLC; Retired, Vice President and General Counsel, The J.M. Smucker Company

M. Ann (Ann) Harlan is a founder and co-chief executive officer of Harlan Peterson Partners, LLC, an executive leadership development firm with a unique focus on client development and professional development consulting. Prior to founding Harlan Peterson Partners, Ann served as vice president, general counsel, and corporate secretary for The J.M. Smucker Company, a NYSE traded company and a leading manufacturer of food products, during which time sales grew from $300 million to $5 billion through a combination of organic growth and transformational acquisitions. Ann has served on the board of directors for The Gorman Rupp Company since 2009, where she is currently the Lead Director and chairs the Nominating and Governance Committee and serves on the Audit Committee. She also previously served on the board of directors of Eatem Foods Company until its sale to Archer Daniels Midland in 2015. Ann also sits on the Advisory Board of Gates Group Capital Partners, is the chair of the board of The First Tee of Cleveland, and is a member of the board of directors for University Hospitals Health System, where she is vice chair of the Compensation Committee and serves on the Audit Committee and the Nominating and Governance Committee.

CARLA HARRIS
Vice Chairman, Wealth Management; Managing Director,
and Senior Client Advisor, Morgan Stanley

Carla Harris is a Vice Chairman, Wealth Management, and Managing Director and Senior Client Advisor at Morgan Stanley. Before being named to her current roles, she headed the Emerging Manager Platform and was also responsible for Equity Private Placements. For more than a decade, she was a senior member of the equity syndicate desk and executed such transactions as initial public offerings for UPS, Martha Stewart Living Omnimedia, Ariba, and Redback. Carla is the immediate past chair of the board of the Morgan Stanley Foundation and the Food Bank of NYC, and sits on the boards of The Executive Leadership Council, Sponsors for Educational Opportunity, A Better Chance, Inc., and Xavier University. In 2013, she was appointed by President Barack Obama to chair the National Women's Business Council, and was recently named to *Fortune Magazine's* list of "The 50 Most Powerful Black Executives in Corporate America" and U.S. Bankers Top 25 Most Powerful Women in Finance (2009, 2010, 2011). She is an active member of the St. Charles Gospelites of the St. Charles Borromeo Catholic Church and the Mark Howell Singers, and has released several gospel albums. She is also the author of *Expect to Win* and *Strategize to Win*.

E. LAVERNE JOHNSON
Founder, President, and Chief Executive Officer, International Institute for Learning, Inc.

E. LaVerne (LaVerne) Johnson is founder, president, and chief executive officer of International Institute for Learning, Inc. (IIL), a leading global corporate training and consulting company headquartered in New York City, with 18 wholly owned companies around the world. IIL was founded in 1991 by LaVerne, who has a Master's degree in Finance and Economics from Michigan State University. She has been called one of the most powerful leaders in project management by the Project Management Institute, and recently received special recognition from the PMI Educational Foundation as a PMIEF Mission Partner for IIL's donation of $1 million to fund a Project Management Skills for Life curriculum, plus four academic scholarships every year, available to graduate and undergraduate students studying project management at degree-granting colleges and universities.

ERIKA KARP
Founder and Chief Executive Officer, Cornerstone Capital Inc.

Prior to founding Cornerstone Capital Inc. in 2013, Erika Karp was managing director and head of global sector research for UBS Investment Bank, where she chaired the UBS Global Investment Review Committee and managed a global team of analysts and strategists. Cornerstone Capital aims to apply the principles of sustainable finance across capital markets and enhance investment processes through transparency and collaboration. Erika is an advisor to the UN Global Compact's LEAD Board Development Program, a founding board member of the Sustainability Accounting Standards Board, and a member of the World Economic Forum's Global Agenda Council on Financing and Capital. She was named among the nation's "Top 50 Women in Wealth" by AdvisorOne and one of the 50 "Conscious Capitalists" who are "Transforming Wall Street."

ROBIN M. KILBRIDE
President, Chief Executive Officer, and Chairman of the Board, Smithers-Oasis Company

Robin began her career at Smithers-Oasis in 1983 as a senior financial analyst, was named to controller in 1987, chief financial officer in 2001, executive vice president in 2005, president and chief operations officer in 2006, and president and chief executive officer in 2011 after leading a management buyout of the company. She was elected chairman of the board in 2014. Robin currently serves on the boards and committees of several private companies and non-profit organizations, including Ball Horticultural Company, Kent State University, and Wadsworth United Methodist Church.

ILENE H. LANG
Former President and Chief Executive Officer, Catalyst

Ilene Lang is broadly recognized as a pioneering female high-tech/internet executive, having founded AltaVista Internet Software Inc. and serving as senior vice president at Lotus Development Corporation before becoming president and chief executive officer at Catalyst. During her tenure at Catalyst, Ilene helped double revenue, triple membership, quadruple brand awareness, and increase the number of research reports and knowledge products tenfold. To honor her legacy, Catalyst established the Lang Legacy Fund, an individual giving program to sustain the growth she directed and honor her impact on the world of women and business. In 2013, Ilene was awarded the Foreign Policy Association Medal, and named to the National Association of Corporate Directors Hall of Fame in 2014.

BETH E. MOONEY
Chairman and Chief Executive Officer, KeyCorp

Beth Mooney served in several roles at KeyCorp before being elected Chairman and Chief Executive Officer in 2011. She has more than 30 years of experience in retail banking, commercial lending, and real estate financing. Before joining KeyCorp in 2006, Beth held senior-level positions at AmSouth Bancorporation, Bank One Corporation, and Citicorp Real Estate, Inc. A recipient of numerous awards, Beth has been recognized by *Forbes Magazine* as one of "The World's 100 Most Powerful Women" and one of the Top 50 "Most Powerful Women in Business" by *Fortune Magazine* several times. In 2015, she was named the #1 Most Powerful Woman in Banking for the third year in a row by *American Banker*.

DENISE MORRISON
President and Chief Executive Officer, Campbell Soup Company

Denise Morrison has spent more than 30 years in the food industry, including eight years at Campbell Soup Company (in several senior positions) before being named president and chief executive officer in 2011. Before joining Campbell's, Denise was executive vice president and general manager of Kraft Foods' Snacks and Confections divisions, and before that, held leadership roles at Nabisco, Nestle, and Pepsi-Cola. Denise serves on the board of directors for MetLife, and was appointed co-chair of the Consumer Goods Forum in 2015 while also serving on their board. She was named to President Barack Obama's Export Council in 2012 and is a founding member of the Healthy Weight Commitment Foundation. She is also a member of the board of directors for the Grocery Manufacturers Association and Catalyst, and is regularly named among *Fortune* and *Forbes'* Most Powerful Women.

KAREN PARKHILL
Executive Vice President and Chief Financial Officer, Medtronic

Karen Parkhill was named executive vice president and chief financial officer for Medtronic in May 2016. She previously served as vice chairman and chief financial officer for Comerica Incorporated for five years. Karen has more than 25 years of financial experience, including nearly 20 years at JP Morgan Chase where she served in various roles in investment banking as well as chief financial officer for the commercial banking business before joining Comerica. Karen is a member of the International Women's Forum, serves as a National Trustee for the Boys and Girls Club of America, and is a member of the board of directors for the Methodist Health System in Dallas. She was named one of the "Top 25 Most Powerful Women in Banking" by *American Banker Magazine* in 2015.

SANDRA PIANALTO
Former President and Chief Executive Officer, Federal Reserve Bank of Cleveland

Sandra Pianalto began her career at the Federal Reserve Bank of Cleveland in 1983 as an economist, and moved through the ranks to be named president and chief executive officer in 2003 until 2014. During her tenure, she participated in the formulation of U.S. monetary policy and led more than 1,000 employees in Cleveland, Cincinnati, and Pittsburgh in their work of conducting economic research, supervising financial institutions, and providing payment services to commercial banks and the U.S. government. Sandra currently serves on the boards of Eaton Corporation, The J.M. Smucker Company, Prudential Financial, Inc., and is Chair of the Board of University Hospitals. She is also an Advisory Trustee and an Executive in Residence at The University of Akron.

DR. JEAN ROGERS
Chief Executive Officer and Founder, Sustainability Accounting Standards Board

Dr. Jean Rogers founded the Sustainability Accounting Standards Board (SASB) in 2010 from an idea that formulated in collaboration with the Harvard University Initiative for Responsible Investment. Prior to founding SASB, Jean served as a principal at Arup, a global engineering firm focused on sustainable development and was a management consultant at Deloitte, working in the environmental and manufacturing practices. Jean is a former Loeb Fellow at Harvard University, and was named one of the Top 100 Most Influential People in Accounting by *Accounting Today* in 2015.

MARCELLA KANFER ROLNICK
Vice Chair, GOJO

Marcella Kanfer Rolnick focuses on creating meaning and value through her diverse family enterprise—including GOJO, the global leader in skin health and hygiene solutions for away-from-home markets and inventor of PURELL® Hand Sanitizer, and an array of early-stage ventures and philanthropic foundations. At GOJO, Marcella ensures preconditions for long-term viability and vitality are in place; this includes her championship of sustainability, innovation, and organizational effectiveness. She co-founded and guides Walnut Ridge Strategic Management Company, a management and administration services provider.

Throughout her career, Marcella has performed numerous roles within GOJO, including establishing the e-business practice and launching new markets. She has also worked in management consulting, nonprofit business development, and investment advisory services. Marcella serves on various boards, including EP Technologies, UNKNWN, Meeteor, The Fowler Center for Business as an Agent of World Benefit, American Jewish World Service, and Lippman Kanfer Foundation for Living Torah. Marcella was named one of Jewish Women International's 10 "Women to Watch" and *Crain's Cleveland Business'* "Forty Under 40." Marcella received the "Woman of the Year" Award for Innovation by the Women's History Project of the Akron Area. Marcella, her husband, and four children reside in Brooklyn, NY; Akron, OH; and Chautauqua, NY.

LISA SHERMAN
President and Chief Executive Officer, The Advertising Council

Lisa Sherman is President and CEO of the Ad Council, the national non-profit behind the most impactful public service campaigns in the U.S., including Smokey Bear, "Friends Don't Let Friends Drive Drunk" and the recent viral phenomenon "Love Has No Labels." In this position, she leverages her extensive experience in molding and leading national communications programs with her strong passion for social causes. Lisa harnesses more than 20 years of experience as a leader and innovator in the communications industry. Previously with Viacom, she launched LogoTV, the leading entertainment network aimed at the LBGT community. She has also served as EVP at Hill, Holliday Connors, Cosmopulos, and held a number of executive and senior-level marketing, advertising, and operating positions at Verizon Communications. Lisa's commitment to social good is also evident outside the office where she serves as the Vice Chair of the Board of God's Love We Deliver and on the Advisory Board of TMI, the consulting arm of DoSomething.org. She has been recognized with awards including *Ad Age's* "Women to Watch 2015" and Big Brothers Big Sisters of NYC's Public Service Award in 2016. Lisa is an inductee into the YWCA's Academy of Women Leaders and a Metzger-Conway fellow at her alma mater, Dickinson College.

BARBARA R. SNYDER
President, Case Western Reserve University

President of Case Western Reserve University since 2007, Snyder has encouraged interdisciplinary excellence, catalyzed institutional collaboration, and reinvigorated alumni engagement and fundraising. For example, in 2013, Case Western Reserve entered into a historic partnership with Cleveland Clinic to develop a Health Education Campus including the university's schools of medicine, nursing, and dental medicine and broke ground in fall 2015.

During Snyder's tenure, the university has tripled undergraduate applications, become twice as selective, and dramatically improved the academic credentials of the entering class. The university also reached its $1 billion capital campaign goal early and expanded it to $1.5 billion.

Snyder graduated from the University of Chicago Law School and earned her bachelor's degree from The Ohio State University. Prior to becoming president of Case Western Reserve, she was executive vice president and provost at Ohio State. Snyder is a director of the Association of American Universities, American Council on Education, Business-Higher Education Forum, Greater Cleveland Partnership, JobsOhio, and a trustee of Internet2. She is also a director of KeyCorp and Progressive Corporation. She is a member of the Ohio Business Roundtable and an elected member of the American Law Institute.

DARLA STUCKEY
President and Chief Executive Officer, Society for Corporate Governance

Darla Stuckey joined the Society for Corporate Governance in 2009 and was named president and chief executive officer in 2015. She has testified before the House Financial Services Committee on Dodd-Frank governance issues, and is a sought-after speaker on important legal, policy, advocacy, and research issues. Prior to joining the Society for Corporate Governance, Darla was Senior Assistant Secretary at American Express Company and Corporate Secretary at the New York Stock Exchange.

DR. JERRY SUE THORNTON
Chief Executive Officer, Dream/Catcher Educational Consulting Service

Dream/Catcher Educational Consulting Service is a consulting firm that provides coaching and professional development for newly selected college and university presidents. Dr. Jerry Sue Thornton served as president of Cuyahoga Community College (Tri-C) from 1992 until retiring as president emeritus in 2013. Before joining Cuyahoga Community College, Dr. Thornton served as president of Lakewood Community College in Minnesota from 1985 to 1991. She also held several senior-level leadership positions at Triton College (Illinois). In 2011, Dr. Thornton was appointed co-chair of the 21st Century Commission on the Future of Community Colleges, a national task force convened by the American Association of Community Colleges. She currently serves on the boards of University Hospitals Health System and the Rock and Roll Hall of Fame and Museum. She serves on several corporate boards including FirstEnergy Corporation, Applied Industrial Technologies, Inc., Barnes and Noble Education, Inc., and Republic Powdered Metals, Inc. (RPM, Inc.). She was inducted into the Ohio Women's Hall of Fame in 1999 and recognized annually by Northern Ohio Live as one of the Top Women Professionals. She received the American Association of Community Colleges Leadership Award in 2014.

LISA WOLL
Chief Executive Officer, US SIF/ US SIF Foundation

Lisa Woll has worked as an advocate and organization-builder across a range of domestic and international issues. She has been the chief executive officer of US SIF: The Forum for Sustainable and Responsible Investment and the US SIF Foundation for a decade, and has been advancing sustainable and impact investing through high-quality research, programming, education, convenings, and through engagement with the media and policymakers. Before US SIF, Lisa was executive director of the International Women's Media Foundation, an organization focused on press freedom and expansion of women's role in the media. She was the director of the first international study to look at the impact of the Convention on the Rights of the Child and directed the Washington, DC office of Save the Children. She is the founder of Suited for Change, a Washington, DC-based nonprofit organization serving low-income women, and a co-founder of The Women's Alliance and Advantage Ethiopia: Kid's Tennis and Education Fund. She has a Master's degree in Women's Studies and her motto is "Don't agonize, organize."

....

MARGARET W. WONG
Managing Partner, Margaret W. Wong & Associates, LLC

Margaret Wong is an award-winning managing partner of her namesake law firm, bringing more than 38 years of experience in immigration and nationality law and legal practice management to her valued clients. Margaret W. Wong & Associates is nationally and internationally renowned for its ability to successfully represent clients and companies in obtaining immigration status. Her firm is rated AV Preeminent, is a Best Lawyers' Best Law Firm, and is rated 10 by AVVO. Margaret is a sought-after speaker and author, is an adjunct professor at Case Western Reserve University Law School and Founding Chair of the seminar on immigration and naturalization law of the Federal Bar Association, Northern District of Ohio. Her law firm has won more than 35 precedent-setting cases in U.S. Federal Courts and Boards of Immigration Appeals. She was also named Honor Professor of People at the University of China (China's top law school) and is the author of *The Immigrant's Way*. She sat on Ohio Senator Sherrod Brown's Ad Hoc Committee on Nominations of U.S. Attorneys and U.S. Marshals of the Southern District of Ohio. She loves reading and writing. She has represented thousands of immigrants throughout her life, and she personally sees more than 100 clients most weeks of her working life.

JACQUELINE WOODS
Retired President, AT&T Ohio

Jacqueline (Jackie) Woods is the retired president of AT&T Ohio and was the first woman to be president of a major public utility company where she oversaw the transformation from a regulated utility to a consumer-driven competitive communication company. Jackie currently serves on the board of directors for The Timken Company and The Andersons Inc., and formerly on the boards of School Specialty and Office Max. She is a former board chair and trustee of Kent State University; a trustee of Muskingum University, University Hospitals Case Medical Center, and the Cleveland Bluecoats; and is a national trustee of the Association of Governing Boards. During her career Jackie has served on over 20 civic and non-profit boards; is a chair emeritus of the Greater Cleveland Chapter of the American Red Cross and Great Lakes Science Center; and has received numerous awards including the YWCA Lifetime Achievement Award (2008), Athena Award (2009), was inducted into the Northeast Ohio Inside Business Hall of Fame in 2010, and most recently won The Cleveland Foundation Women of Note Legacy Award.